TOTAL
RECOVERY

TOTAL RECOVERY

SUPERNATURAL RESTORATION
AND RELEASE

BENNY HINN

CLARION CALL MARKETING

DALLAS, TEXAS

CONTENTS

INTRODUCTION:
DAVID'S 3-D ARMY

David therefore departed thence, and escaped to the cave Adullam and when his brethren and all his father's house heard it, they went down thither to him. And every one that was in distress, and every one that was in debt, and everyone that was discontented, gathered themselves unto him; and he became a captain over them: and there were with him about four hundred men.

—1 SAMUEL 22:1–2

Three tragic words literally jump out of the passage above: *distress*, *debt*, and *discontented*. Everyone in David's ragtag band of soldiers suffered from these three overwhelming challenges.

A comparison of the 3-D collection of riffraff described in 1 Samuel 22 to the awe-inspiring army found in 1 Samuel 30 must surely be one of the most amazing transformations of any group in history.

What is the story behind the massive change? More important, how can we harness that transforming power to revolutionize our lives today?

A quick look into the background of this scripture shows how David, already anointed by the prophet Samuel to be the next king of

Israel and already a celebrated hero for his victory over the giant Goliath, suddenly was faced with circumstances that forced him and his small band to flee for their lives.

It seems Saul didn't enjoy the way things were going. People on the street were singing songs about the young warrior (1 Samuel 18). Even Saul's son Jonathan had sided with David (1 Samuel 20). Soon Saul's dissatisfaction with the situation turned to jealousy. Blinded by his rage, Saul made plans to destroy David and thereby regain the kingdom's loyalty and praise.

David, warned by Jonathan, ended up in a cave. It must have been a rather large cavern, for he was joined by a strange band of 400 followers, the original 3-D army.

Why do I call it the 3-D army? It has nothing to do with the movies of the 1950s and 1960s which required everyone to wear paper and plastic glasses. Remember those?

No, it has nothing to do with cinema. Instead, it has to do with the characteristics of David's ragtag band of soldiers. All of them were apparently in trouble. The Bible specifically records three specific challenges every one of them faced: distress, debt, and discontent.

Many in this 3-D army were David's own relatives. I can tell you with great certainty that it was not a group most people would like to captain. In fact, I'm not sure there is a pastor in the world who would knowingly accept the call to a church consisting of 400 people who are fomenting with distress, debt, and discontent.

So, what did David do? We don't know every single word he said during the coming weeks and months, but we do know that David began preaching a message of victory and recovery.

How do we know that?

Powerful, Life-Changing Words

Take a look through the Psalms. That was David's God-inspired journal and songbook. It was composed during the best and worst of times.

The first sentence of the Psalms starts with the word *blessed*:

> *Blessed is the man that walketh not in the counsel of the ungodly, nor standeth in the way of sinners, nor sitteth in the seat of the scornful. But his delight is in the law of the Lord; and in his law doeth he meditate day and night. And he shall be like a tree planted by the rivers of water, that bringeth forth his fruit in his season; his leaf also shall not wither; and whatsoever he doeth shall prosper.* (Psalm 1:1–4)

Over and over as David faced challenges against overwhelming odds, he found a way to keep himself from joining in with the 3-D chorus. At the same time, he was able to point his unlikely band of soldiers toward a better future.

In fact, in 1 Samuel 30 an amazing story of restoration and abundance unfolds: *"David encouraged himself in the LORD his God…and David inquired at the LORD, saying, shall I pursue after this troop? shall I over take them? And he answered him, Pursue: for thou shalt surely overtake them, and without fail recover all"* (verses 6 and 8).

What happened between the accounts recorded in 1 Samuel 20 and 30 to make such a profound difference? Whatever it was, David came to the glorious place where he could write:

> *The Lord is my shepherd; I shall not want.…He restoreth my soul. . . . Yea, though I walk through the valley of the shadow of death, I will fear no evil: for thou art with me.… Thou preparest*

a table before me in the presence of mine enemies: thou anoin-
test my head with oil; my cup runneth over. (Psalm 23:1, 3–5)

God's will for David was to recover everything that he lost. In the midst of David's crises, even when people failed him, when unjust things happened, and even after the enemy stole everything from him, he was able to recover all.

I believe we are safe in assuming that David began preaching his message of recovery and victory to his little 3-D band. You see, as we move beyond 1 Samuel, within one generation the country was literally overrun with abundance. According to 2 Chronicles 1:15, by the time Solomon became king of Israel, silver and gold were as plenteous as stones.

Can you imagine? Through this time of major transformation, the land became a place where precious metals were as common as rocks. God used David to build a powerful, victorious nation out of a small band of people who had once been mired in distress, debt, and discouragement.

TOTAL RECOVERY TODAY

Total recovery can be as much a part of our Christian world in the twenty-first century as it was in David's time. There are many marvelous passages in God's Word that establish the fact that God has promised restoration and abundance.

You see, recovery is not something for which we merely hope. It is the promise of God! Whether we understand and apply these principles of recovery or not, God has made them available to us.

What does it mean to experience this kind of restoration and abundance? It means that you regain all that has been stolen from you through the eternal work of the One with the name above every name—the Lord Jesus. Through Him you regain your strength, are restored to health, are rescued from destruction, become established in God's kingdom, and are made new. Lost time is redeemed. You are refreshed, replenished, revived. You recover all!

Joel 2:23–26 contains a glorious promise that is as potent and powerful for today's believers as it was when it was given:

> *Be glad then, ye children of Zion, and rejoice in the LORD your God: for he hath given you the former rain moderately, and he will cause to come down for you the rain, the former rain, and the latter rain in the first month. And the floors shall be full of wheat, and the fats shall overflow with wine and oil. And I will restore to you the years that the locust hath eaten, the cankerworm, and the caterpiller, and the palmerworm, my great army which I sent among you. And ye shall eat in plenty, and be satisfied, and praise the name of the LORD your God, that hath dealt wondrously with you: and my people shall never be ashamed.*

Restoration! Overflow! Plenty! God's will is that you lack nothing good in your life. I believe with all of my heart that is exactly what God has promised.

It is up to us as His people to prepare our lives for total recovery by increasing our capacity to receive God's abiding and abundant grace. It is also up to us to spend enough time with Him to understand how our definition of "good" is often much different from what God's true goodness really is.

THE GOD OF RECOVERY

Throughout God's dealing with the human race, we see repeatedly that the Lord is the God of recovery. Certainly, when God the Father gave His Son, the Lord Jesus, to die as a sacrifice for our sin, He determined that His children should recover all.

When you made the decision to give your life to Christ Jesus, old things passed away and all things became new. As you take on His life, you receive abundant life. The Word of God even says that Jesus is able to do *"exceeding abundantly above"* all that you could ask or think *"according to the power"* that works in you (Ephesians 3:20).

The Lord has given many great and precious promises to us dealing with recovery—from Abraham to the children of Israel, from Job to the prodigal son, from the widow of Zarephath (who fed Elijah the last of her food) to blind Bartimaeus. In each instance, when all seemed lost, God restored abundantly and supernaturally.

Still, so many Christians have only scratched the surface of understanding total recovery and how to obtain it. We spend so much time looking back at what we lost, or we focus so much on our future in heaven, and we neglect what God desires for us right now!

Kathryn Kuhlman used to say, "The saddest thing is going to be for some people, when they get to heaven and find out how much they missed here."

One day in heaven, we will experience the complete fullness of God, but it is important not to overlook that God wants you to be blessed here on earth right now. The Lord's will is to see you whole, your life restored, and all that you have lost totally recovered.

God's Word—the Book of Recovery

From beginning to end, the Bible itself is a book of recovery. God created man and woman in abundance and placed them in a marvelous garden where they had all they could ever want or need, yet they fell away from the Lord and began to live in sin. Adam lost all; and Christ came to recover what was lost.

Your own life is also a story of recovery. Once you were lost and now you are found. Once you were blind and now you can see. Your own testimony is a story of recovery. The second you were born again, you came under the law of resurrection and you were delivered from the law of destruction.

The Lord has already performed the promises in His Word for you. So why should recovery be a foreign thing to you? God's love is so great for you that He has been leading you toward total recovery even while you did not know how much you needed to be rescued from sin and destruction.

Charles Finney, one of the great Christian evangelists and writers of the 1800s, spoke with powerful conviction when he said: "God's love is not based on His being satisfied with us or having a high opinion of us. There is no basis in us for such a love. Thus, God's love can be nothing but the love of unselfish benevolence."[1]

In God's great mercy, He brought you and me out of darkness and into light, out of sickness and into health, out of bondage and into liberty. That is recovery, and it is time that you, as God's child, keep going forward in this powerful, miraculous life. The Lord has so much more that He wants to add to you each day!

The Promise of Total Recovery

The Word of God promises that *"blessings shall come on thee, and overtake thee"* (Deuteronomy 28:2). Yet we have embraced so little of what God has promised. We must begin to think the way God wants us to think and receive His promises in our lives.

God's people are a mighty people. We are not a ragtag 3-D army! We must get the world's thinking of loss and lack out of our minds. As a Christian, you are under a completely different umbrella or covering than those who have not accepted the Lord Jesus in their lives.

We are not the devil's slaves. We don't have to live on a bare existence of negativity, defeat, sickness, and loss. Ephesians 4:23–24 points this out: *"Be renewed in the spirit of your mind; And that ye put on the new man, which after God is created in righteousness and true holiness."*

We are not cowering in darkness. We are standing in the light of great glory. God's blessing of total recovery is ours by promise!

The Law of Life

Since the day you became a Christian, the power of God has been working in you to reverse what the devil has stolen. First Corinthians 15:22 says, *"For as in Adam all die, even so in Christ shall all be made alive."* Adam was created by God to stay alive, yet Adam went from life to death, and since then all men have gone from life to death.

Christ wants to reverse the process. Through Him, we move from death to life: *"For the law of the Spirit of life in Christ Jesus hath made me free from the law of sin and death"* (Romans 8:2).

God's children live under a set of rules different from the world's. The world's system says that everything born must die. God says everything that dies will live. The world says everything starts out new and then it gets old. God says the old can become new. The world says everything strong becomes weak. God says everything weak can become strong. In fact, scientists universally agree that we live in an ever-expanding universe, more new than old.

We serve the God who makes all things new! The world goes from light to darkness, but God says, "From darkness, I will make light."

The world goes from liberty to bondage, but God says that we go from bondage to liberty. When you come under the influence of the Holy Ghost, you come under the influence of the law of new life. The old man is put off and the new man is put on.

The world says full becomes empty, but God says empty becomes full. When you come to God, you are empty, and He fills you up! If you go to the devil full, he will pour what you already have out of you, and he will empty you out.

God did not intend for the strong to become weak, for the light to become dark, and for the healthy to become sick. God ordained that the negative become positive, not the other way around. Adam brought the negative through sin, and Christ brought the positive through the work of the cross.

Lost and Found

When you are in Christ, you tap into a positive power working in your life. As a Christian, God's power affects your life in such a way that you are actually turned around.

Before you gave your life to the Lord, you were going one way and being pulled in one direction by an evil force. That evil force pulls people from life to death, light to darkness, and freedom to bondage. When Jesus entered your life, God said you would now go from darkness to light, sickness to health, bondage to liberty, and weakness to strength. Psalm 30:11 says, *"Thou hast turned for me my mourning into dancing."*

For the Christian, recovery is a process that begins in Jesus Christ. It is for you today! As your life is filled with God's Word, and you act upon your faith, you will have the authority to take back or regain what has been stolen from you. It is your legal right to reclaim what belongs to you.

The law of God concerning a thief is clear in the Bible, and the Word tells us that Satan is a thief. Therefore, the law of God applies to him regarding what has been stolen from you. Exodus 22:3 says a thief shall restore and *"make full restitution."*

The devil must make full restitution for what he has stolen from you. That is the law of God, and the devil must obey it. The Word of God says, *"If the thief be found, let him pay double"* (Exodus 22:7). The enemy must pay you back double for what you have lost.

It is time we subpoena the devil and bring an indictment against him, find him guilty, and force him to restore everything in the name of Jesus. Our God is the God of the lost and found. This is your day to find and recover what you have lost!

A FINAL NOTE

What does it mean to experience total recovery? It means that you regain all that has been stolen from you, and more!

As with David, you can discover these life-changing principles as you overcome the three *D*s of distress, debt, and discontent. On the following pages you will learn how to

- Develop the four *P*s of praise, prayer, pursuit, and power;

- Equip yourself with the biblical weapons of war;

- Discover the authority you have been given to take back what the enemy of your soul has taken;

- Reclaim your family;

- Unleash the floodgates of God's blessing in your life.

The three profound words from 1 Samuel 30:19—*"David recovered all"*—should cause great faith to rise in the heart of every believer. You can start your own move toward total recovery as you enter into a new dimension of faith and blessing from this moment forward!

1

GOD'S PLAN FOR
TOTAL RECOVERY

The LORD is my shepherd; I shall not want. He maketh me to lie down in green pastures: he leadeth me beside the still waters. He restoreth my soul: he leadeth me in the paths of righteousness for his name's sake. Yea, though I walk through the valley of the shadow of death, I will fear no evil: for thou art with me; thy rod and thy staff they comfort me. Thou preparest a table before me in the presence of mine enemies: thou anointest my head with oil; my cup runneth over. Surely goodness and mercy shall follow me all the days of my life: and I will dwell in the house of the LORD for ever.

—PSALM 23

David lost everything except His faith, yet he recovered all. God's recovery, restoration, and abundance that the psalmist came to know throughout his life is expressed in Psalm 23. David, under the Holy Spirit's direction, was able to pen those words because he had experienced firsthand a dramatic turning point in his life. It is 1 Samuel 30 that marks one of the major turning points in David's life.

David did not come into the glorious place where he could say *"my cup runneth over"* until he discovered God's plan for recovery. After that turning point, David was able to begin reigning. After King Saul's death, recorded in 1 Samuel 31, David took the throne of Israel. The restoration was complete.

Total recovery can be as much a part of your world today as it was for David. You can regain all that has been stolen from you. You can regain your strength, be restored to health, be rescued from destruction, become established in God's kingdom, and be made new. You can be redeemed. You can be refreshed, replenished, and revived. You can recover all!

Nothing is lost when you serve God. The Lord Jesus promised that *"every one that hath forsaken houses, or brethren, or sisters, or father, or mother, or wife, or children, or lands, for my name's sake, shall receive an hundredfold, and shall inherit everlasting life"* (Matthew 19:29). God will command His blessings upon you when your commitment to Him is steadfast and true.

God said that if you serve Him, *"He shall bless thy bread and thy water; and I will take sickness away from the midst of thee"* (Exodus 23:25). As you abide in Christ, God will multiply everything you touch, keep your children safe, watch over your home, and drive the enemy away from you.

How do we know this? God's Word provides illustration after illustration of restoration and abundance.

Job's Recovery

Think about Job, for example, who thought that he lost everything, yet he recovered all and more. Even though Job was at his lowest point, he prayed, *"I know that thou canst do every thing, and that no thought can be withholden from thee"* (Job 42:2).

Job's trust in the Lord remained strong and true despite his circumstances. The Lord was pleased with Job, and nothing was lost by him: *"And the LORD turned the captivity of Job, when he prayed for his friends: also the LORD gave Job twice as much as he had before"* (Job 42:10).

The Word of God goes on to say, *"The LORD blessed the latter end of Job more than his beginning"* (Job 42:12). What looked like a loss in Job's life really was not a loss at all. In fact, because Job trusted in the Lord, God gave him more in the end than he had in the beginning.

PETER'S RECOVERY

We also see an example of total recovery and restoration in the life of Peter. It was Peter's decision to deny Christ, yet less than a hundred days later he preached on the Day of Pentecost and 3,000 people were born again. Peter denied the Lord, yet he recovered all. The Lord did not reject Peter even when Peter denied Him three times.

Instead, after the Savior's resurrection, Peter saw the Lord on the shore from the boat. Jesus was busy cooking Peter's breakfast. Peter jumped into the water and rushed over to Jesus. There is much more to this story than just a meal.

Why did Jesus cook breakfast for Peter? The Jews believed that meals reconciled people with one another; a meal said, "I accept you." If you eat with someone it means that you accept him. When Peter saw Jesus cooking his breakfast, he did not have to ask another question. He knew he was accepted and that Jesus had forgiven him, for we do not eat meals with an enemy.

Even today, sharing a meal with someone allows healing to occur. Jesus showed Peter that he was accepted and that everything was all right. Jesus did not mention a word about the mistake that Peter had made while they shared their meal. Instead, Jesus said, *"Lovest thou me?"* Peter answered, *"Yea, Lord; thou knowest that I love thee."* Jesus replied to him, *"Feed my lambs"* (John 21:15).

The Lord was saying, "I have not changed my mind about you, Peter. The call to ministry has not left you. All is well." Peter was totally accepted and forgiven by the Lord. Recovery and restoration came with the forgiveness.

The Prodigal Son's Recovery

The New Testament story of the young man who went astray is another example. He lost everything because of his own mistakes, yet he recovered all when he returned to his father. There came a point in the prodigal son's life where he realized the mistake he had made. The Bible says the prodigal son *"came to himself"* and asked, *"How many hired servants of my father's have bread enough and to spare, and I perish with hunger!"* (Luke 15:17). He decided he would return to his father and repent for what he had done. What happened next is remarkable:

> *And he arose, and came to his father. But when he was yet a great way off, his father saw him, and had compassion, and ran, and fell on his neck, and kissed him. And the son said unto him, Father, I have sinned against heaven, and in thy sight, and am no more worthy to be called thy son. But the father said to his servants, Bring forth the best robe, and put it on him; and put a ring on his hand, and shoes on his feet: And bring hither the fatted calf, and kill it; and let us eat, and be merry: For this my son was dead, and is alive again; he was lost, and is found. And they began to be merry.* (Luke 15:20–24)

Can you relate to the prodigal son's story? What have you lost financially? Physically? In your family?

You may have believed that what you lost was gone forever, but it doesn't have to be that way. Ephesians 4:23 promises that you can *"be renewed in the spirit of your mind."* You can choose to receive God's grace, unmerited favor, and total recovery regardless of what was lost or how it was lost.

If God put something in your hands, God wants it back in your hands. What legally belongs to you does not belong in the hands of a thief, even if it is partially or fully your fault that it got there. Jesus did not change His mind about Peter when Peter made a mistake, and the Lord has not changed His mind about you over your mistakes. As the prodigal son returned to his earthly father, you can return to your heavenly Father.

Your Recovery

You might wonder about some of the things you have lost saying, "It was my own fault that I lost them. I understand that the Lord will restore what the thief has stolen, but I lost some things in my life due to my own sin."

The Bible makes it clear that God keeps no record of wrongs: *"He hath not dealt with us after our sins; nor rewarded us according to our iniquities. For as the heaven is high above the earth, so great is his mercy toward them that fear him. As far as the east is from the west, so far hath he removed our transgressions from us"* (Psalm 103:10–12).

God can bring total recovery to you, even when it is your own fault that you have experienced loss. Charles Spurgeon, England's best-known preacher for most of the second half of the nineteenth century, once said: "We are perfectly accepted in Christ, and not partial. It does not go to a limited extent, but goes the whole way. Our unrighteousness is covered. From condemnation we are entirely and irrevocably free."[1]

No matter what you have done or what mistakes you have made, the Lord will forgive you. Your meal of acceptance and recovery are found in God's Word, which provides *"life unto those that find them, and health to all their flesh"* (Proverbs 4:22). You may think you have lost everything, but as my dear friend Richard Roberts says often, "God is the God of the second chance!"

If you missed it the first time, God will bring it around the second time and help you the next time not to miss it. As Christians, we operate under a different set of rules. We are not under the law of destruction. We are under the law of resurrection. The world lives in the negative, but we live in the positive. Everything the world lays its hands on dies, but everything God lays His hands on lives. When the world tries to influence you, it takes away from you; but when God's power pours into your life, He forgives, accepts, blesses, brings increase, and helps you recovery.

When you are under the umbrella of God's power, you are in drive, not reverse. In Christ, everything about you goes forward, not backward. The moment you come under the umbrella of God's presence, the very second you are in Christ, everything about you begins to recover. Restoration is the outcome of the life of Christ in you.

John 10:10 relates: *"I am come that they might have life, and that they might have it more abundantly."* The life that Jesus gave you is within itself recovery and gain.

Ongoing, Expanding Recovery

The Christian life is an ever-expanding life moving from life into deeper life. One translation for this expanding power is *dunamis,* which means power reproducing itself within itself. The power of God causes the Christian life to be a journey of growth that continues to broaden outward and become a blessing to all it touches. It is like light that goes out of one spot and moves in every direction.

Just as light expands, we as Christians are continually expanding. We go from life to doubled life and then from doubled life to quadrupled life. As the power of God touches life, it keeps expanding within the heart until it reaches abundant life, and from there it still continues to grow and expand until eventually it becomes life eternal.

The same principle applies to joy. As you keep God's commandments and abide in His love, His joy will be in you so that your joy will be full. However, joy does not stop there. According to 1 Peter 1:8, you will have *"joy unspeakable and full of glory."* God wants to see you filled to capacity and brimming over with blessings in your life.

The Bible also declares that glory expands within you: *"But we all, with open face beholding as in a glass the glory of the Lord, are changed into the same image from glory to glory, even as by the Spirit of the Lord"* (2 Corinthians 3:18).

Glory will increase in your life as you behold the Lord and become affected by His presence. The process of growth continues until one day you are in eternal glory with the Lord. God wants you to be surrounded with expanding, intensifying, and thickening life, joy, and glory.

We are changed into the image of the Lord continually. Colossians 3:10 says, *"Put on the new man, which is renewed in knowledge after the image of him that created him."* This verse describes moving transformation and ongoing re-creation.

Recovery happens in your life as you come into the flow of the Holy Ghost. As you put on the new man, a river of life will carry you from faith to faith, life to life, light to light, and power to power.

The Holy Spirit will carry you from place to place in God. Eventually, in heaven you will reach the place of fullness and totality, but God wants the recovery process to begin in you right now so you can experience supernatural restoration in this life.

A Final Note

Sadly, some Christians are still in reverse. They do not know that total recovery belongs to them. Recovery and reversal can be described like two rivers. One moves forward and expands in depth, while the other moves backward and becomes shallow. Psalm 46:4-5 speaks of the river of God that is ever expanding and moving forward: *"There is a river, the streams whereof shall make glad the city of God, the holy place of the tabernacles of the most High. God is in the midst of her; she shall not be moved: God shall help her."* The Word of God shows that this river is a place of healing and recovery and invites you to be touched and restored in its waters.

Are you ready to move into that river? Are you ready to recover all? You can apply the same principles David understood. As you do, your life will never be the same!

2

TOTAL RECOVERY
THROUGH PRAISE

O clap your hands, all ye people; shout unto God with the voice of triumph.

—PSALM 47:1

D avid's decision to praise the Lord, even in the midst of his troubles, and even while surrounded by his unlikely 3-D army, became a crucial turning point in his life.

How bad did it get? After the struggles in the cave and the battles with Saul, things kept getting worse. Read this haunting description of how gloomy things got before the dawn broke:

> *And it came to pass, when David and his men were come to Ziklag on the third day, that the Amalekites had invaded the south, and Ziklag, and smitten Ziklag, and burned it with fire; And had taken the women captives, that were therein: they slew not any, either great or small, but carried them away, and went on their way. So David and his men came to the city, and, behold, it was burned with fire; and their wives, and their sons, and their daughters, were taken captives. (1 Samuel 30:1–3)*

21

So much happened to him that it may even be hard for you to identify with David. It is hard to imagine how it must feel to find everything that you loved and cherished is suddenly gone. That is exactly what happened to David, as reported in these verses. He lost everything!

Let's continue with 1 Samuel 30:4: *"Then David and the people that were with him lifted up their voice and wept, until they had no more power to weep."* David and his followers cried until they could cry no more. Have you ever experienced loss to the point where you had no more tears left? There is a time when there is nothing else to do but cry, and let the sorrow come out of you. In times of great loss, benefit comes to the heart as it is loosed from sorrowful emotions.

Fenelon, a respected sixteenth century French writer, said this:

> God doesn't want to discourage you or to spoil you. Embrace the difficult circumstances you find yourself in—even when you feel they will overwhelm you. Allow God to mold you through the events He allows in your life. This will make you flexible toward the will of God. The events of your life are like a furnace for the heart. All your impurities are melted and your old ways are lost.[1]

David experienced emotions that overwhelmed him, and he faced great trouble to the point that he wept with sorrow. But when his crying was done, something mighty happened: *"David was greatly distressed; for the people spake of stoning him...but David encouraged himself in the LORD his God"* (1 Samuel 30:6).

When David remembered to praise God, regardless of the situation, everything began changing.

RECOVERING ALL THROUGH PRAISE

Remember, the Bible does not say that David was just distressed; it says that he was *"greatly distressed."* He was in the lowest place that he could be, and quite possibly at the bleakest point in his whole life.

David was in a desperate place, but David did not focus on his trouble. Instead, he looked at what God could do through it. In other words, he began praising God in the midst of his trouble by encouraging himself in the Lord. It didn't just happen this one time either. In fact, the Psalms are filled with praise and worship, despite his often-dire situations.

The Bible has many such stories. Shadrach, Meshach, and Abednego (Daniel 3) trusted in the Lord. As they praised God in the midst of the fire, the Lord preserved them. People outside the furnace could even see the form of a fourth person—Jesus Himself—inside with the three Hebrews. And when they came out, not even the smell of smoke was upon them. When you begin praising God in the midst of whatever fire you are going through, miracles can happen. He will show up and rescue you!

As we move to the New Testament, we find the account of the apostle Paul (Acts 16). Though Paul and Silas were imprisoned unjustly, they did not look at the circumstances and become defeated. Instead, they began to sing praises in the night. An earthquake struck the area and the chains fell off. Only those who praise God during difficulty experience God's mighty, delivering power.

It is easy to praise God when everything is going well. It is easy to say "with His stripes I am healed" when you are healthy, but when sickness strikes, it is not so easy. It is easy to say, "I am more than a conqueror" when everything is going wonderfully for you and you feel like you are on top of the world.

The question is, can you maintain an attitude of victory when everything seems to go wrong? Trouble is a powerful place to learn the power of praise. Psalm 27:5 says, *"For in the time of trouble he shall hide me in his pavilion: in the secret of his tabernacle shall he hide me; he shall set me up upon a rock."*

Can you praise God when you are mired in trouble?

TYPES OF PRAISE

Praising God, despite your situation or challenges, is more than a mere positive thinking-type exercise or some happy-go-lucky attitude. It is an eternal, sacred communication between you and Almighty God. It is something that we should do willingly, cheerfully, and purposefully. David understood this point completely. He knew several Hebrew words used for praise:

- *Hallal*—This is the most-often-used Hebrew word used to praise God. Our word "hallelujah" comes from this word. *Hallal* means "to boast in, to celebrate, and to talk with excitement about God." The English translation for "hallelujah" literally means "praise Jehovah." Every time you say "hallelujah," you are praising the Lord.

- *Yadah*—This word means "to worship with extended hands." Psalm 134:2 says, *"Lift up your hands in the sanctuary, and bless the Lord."* Extending your hands is an act of praise and worship to the Lord. When the enemy begins to cause everything around you to crumble, you can lift your hands and start celebrating God. Psalm 63:4 says, *"Thus will I bless thee while I live: I will lift up my hands in thy name."*

- *Barach*—This Hebrew word means "to bless, salute and kneel before." *Barach* is the same word that David used in Psalm 103:1, when he declared, *"Bless the LORD, O my soul."* David was saying, *"Barach Adonai,"* or *"Bless the LORD."*

- *Sharu*—This Hebrew word means "to sing unto the Lord." The psalmist said, *"I will praise the LORD according to his righteousness: and will sing praise to the name of the LORD most high"* (Psalm 7:17).

No matter what situation you are in today, you can lift up praises unto the Lord. It's a principle that is absolutely vital for every believer who seeks to rise above life's many challenges. Praise will lead you to into a life of total recovery.

SEVEN GLORIOUS REASONS

Candidly, why praise God? So many people say that it doesn't seem natural to praise God in the midst of pain and heartache. Yet countless wonderful incentives are mentioned throughout the Bible. Here are seven of the most vital reasons for you to begin moving into a deeper dimension of praise:

1. **Praise is where God lives.** When you praise Him, you come to His house. Psalm 22:3 says, *"But thou art holy, O thou that inhabitest the praises of Israel."* God inhabits the praise of Israel. Praise is God's address, so when you praise Him you are coming to where He lives.

2. **Praise is the access you are given into the presence of God.** Psalm 100:4 says, *"Enter into his gates with thanksgiving, and into his courts with praise: be thankful unto him, and bless his*

name." You enter into God's gates with thanksgiving in your heart and into His courts with praise.

3. **Praise is a God-given garment that drives away the spirit of heaviness.** Isaiah 61:3 says that God has given you *"the garment of praise for the spirit of heaviness."* A garment, as the Scripture references here, is a covering against oppression and any burden that tries to weigh you down.

4. **Praise brings deliverance.** Psalm 50:23 says, *"Whoso offereth praise glorifieth me: and to him that ordereth his conversation aright will I shew the salvation of God."* If you want to experience deliverance in your life, you must praise the Lord. The word *salvation* in this verse also means deliverance. Praise breaks the chains that bind you.

5. **Praise brings protection and preservation.** Psalm 59:17 says, *"Unto thee, O my strength, will I sing: for God is my defence, and the God of my mercy."* There is protection in praise, and when you honor the Lord, you will be preserved: *"My praise shall be continually of thee. I am as a wonder unto many; but thou art my strong refuge. Let my mouth be filled with thy praise and with thy honour all the day"* (Psalm 71:6–8).

6. **Praise is an arsenal against your enemies.** Praising God helps you fight the enemy. The Lord is mighty, and when you speak of Him, the devil is constrained. Psalm 149:6–9 points to this clear-cut principle:

Let the high praises of God be in their mouth, and a twoedged sword in their hand; To execute vengeance upon the heathen, and punishments upon the people; To bind their kings with chains, and their nobles with fetters of iron; To execute upon them the judgment written: this honour have all his saints. Praise ye the LORD.

7. **Praise releases God to do battle for you.** We learn in 2 Chronicles 20:22: *"And when they began to sing and to praise, the LORD set ambushments against the children of Ammon, Moab, and mount Seir, which were come against Judah; and they were smitten."*

Throughout the Old Testament, when Israel began to sing and praise God, God began to fight for them. Throughout David's life, when he worshiped and praised the Lord, things began to change. And as you lift your praises to Him, the Lord goes before you, too, to fight on your behalf.

RECOVERY BEGINS INSIDE

David concentrated upon God's promises rather than making his external problems the central point of his focus. Problems come and go all the time—things will always change in your life—and that is why it is so important to lay a foundation of praise.

David wrote Psalm 23, in which he recognized God as his Source for everything: *"The LORD is my shepherd; I shall not want."* David had a proper view of prosperity and life. The already-anointed king of Israel looked openly to God for his provision.

Your victory and recovery must begin internally, within your heart. Praise to God must be the foundation. All transformation is internal, first and foremost. Then the change becomes apparent externally, as well.

When you think about it, it makes sense that all change must come from inside, not from mere external actions. We see the same pattern in the natural realm. Scientists explain that you cannot change an element unless you change its nucleus. In order for a person to change, the nucleus or innermost self must change first.

Knowing this, we should also realize that we cannot change ourselves simply by dealing with outward things. Too often, we seek to transform ourselves by adjusting the external aspects of our lives—our jobs, relationships, and hobbies—thinking these changes will bring growth, happiness, and newness to our lives. Permanent or real change only comes when the center of our being, our inner drives and motivations, undergoes transformation. Praise can bring that kind of change. As you choose to honor and adore Him, He is able to transform you from the inside out.

Look at David. All he had left was his God-given vision that one day he would become king. However, when the events recorded in 1 Samuel 22 occurred, he was leading his tattered 3-D army. There was a good chance that he was about to lose his very life. Still, he praised God. That praise came welling up from deep within. It certainly didn't come as a result of the external circumstances.

There is a time when no one can encourage you like you can encourage yourself, reaching deep inside for God's secret provision. People can talk to you and counsel with you. They can pray for you. Thank God for that external help. But eventually everything comes down to your direct, unfathomable, intimate relationship with the Creator.

When everything seems to be going wrong, remember the benefits and goodness of God. David praised God by saying, *"Bless the LORD, O my soul: and all that is within me, bless his holy name. Bless the LORD, O my soul, and forget not all his benefits"* (Psalm 103:1–2).

Too often people have a horizontal, external viewpoint, not a vertical, internal one. They look around at all the problems—the price of fuel, unemployment statistics, always-fluctuating markets, wars, the Middle East, and crime rates. It is no wonder people wallow in distress, debt, and discontentment. When we look at the worst of things, especially all the external problems, we find things getting worse.

Problems come and go all the time. External things constantly change. That is why it is so important to lay a foundation of praise, an underlying base or support upon which you are grounded. Praise builds the base under you where you can stand strong in faith when trouble comes.

When the doctor gives a bad report, it is natural that your heart is gripped. Just hearing certain medical terms can make you feel like your world has come to an end. Your mind flows with questions instantly. Your world changes.

When faced with disappointing or even devastating news, you must remember this: God is bigger than any words, situations, or forces on earth. What God says in His Word has more authority than anything. Trusting in God's Word is the only thing that will get you through challenges.

It is good to listen to professionals and apply their wisdom, but God's Word must be first and foremost. Your question should be, What does God say about my problem? When you get disturbing medical news, for example, you can know that God's Word declares, *"For I will restore health unto thee, and I will heal thee of thy wounds, saith the LORD"* (Jeremiah 30:17).

Just imagine what would happen in your life if you started believing God's Word and trusting in His authority as much as you place your trust in the words of financial, medical, political, and even religious experts. It is important to know that 2 Corinthians 1:20 says, *"For all the promises of God in him are yea, and in him Amen."* You can count on what God says to you with your whole heart. You don't have to rely on the latest news bulletins for what happens in your life.

Look at David. With loss all around, he encouraged himself in the Lord his God because he believed God's promises of recovery. Psalm 130:5 says, *"I wait for the LORD, my soul doth wait, and in his word do I hope."*

David did not become a prisoner to his difficulty and circumstance. Neither do you if you believe God is your Source.

David made a decision that he would not forget God's Word, no matter what he was going through. He knew that God's Word would quicken him. He said: *"I will never forget thy precepts: for with them thou hast quickened me. I am thine, save me; for I have sought thy precepts. The wicked have waited for me to destroy me: but I will consider thy testimonies"* (Psalm 119:93–95).

When the enemy came to destroy him, David counted on the Lord. He chose to meditate on God's Word.

When the enemy of your soul seeks to steal from you and destroy everything in sight, what should you do? Consider God's promises. The Lord said when the enemy comes in like a flood , God will raise up a standard against him.

The psalmist said, *"My voice shalt thou hear in the morning, O LORD; in the morning will I direct my prayer unto thee, and will look up"* (Psalm 5:3). When trouble comes your way, praise God for His promises and remember His Word.

In those moments, you must remember God's Word says, *"I will never leave thee, nor forsake thee"* (Hebrews 13:5).

When the world forgets you, God does not. He will fulfill His Word in your life. Isaiah 55:11 shares how God's Word will not return void: *"But it shall accomplish"* that which God pleases *"and it shall prosper in the thing"* where God sent it.

The Lord is faithful to watch over His own. David recognized the importance of seeing God as his Source. That's why he chose to praise Him. That foundation in his life allowed him to stand securely upon the Lord Most High. That's why David could write, *"Great is the LORD, and greatly to be praised; and his greatness is unsearchable"* (Psalm 145:3).

Will you praise God regardless of the situation in your life? Praise is a powerful foundation as you move into the supernatural, overflowing, profound dimension of total recovery.

The Power and Promise of Praise

Have you ever experienced times in prayer when it seems like your prayers hit the wall and then come right back at you? Have you ever had a time when your prayer life seemed dull or dead? Have you ever lifted your hands and felt nothing? If so, you are not alone. Most Christians have experienced that at one time or another.

Every believer can tell you of times when they praise God yet feel nothing. Sometimes no words come. It is at that moment when you must begin to speak the promises of God totally in faith.

Sometimes when you first start praising the Lord it feels as if nothing is happening, but do not stop praising Him. Feelings come and go. Praise should not be dependent upon your feelings. Praise is an act of love and worship because of who God is, not because of what you see or how you feel.

The heart is like a fire. It must be kindled. As you begin to hallow and reverence the Lord, a spark will ignite and begin to burn inside you. You may sometimes wonder if the fire within you is dead, but that is not true. That fire may be deep within, hidden underneath mountains of pain and problems, but when you start praising God, a breakthrough will come to you.

Imagine David trying to lead his 3-D army. At one point they wanted to stone him. It couldn't have been easy to praise God, yet David continued. The psalmist understood the power and promise of praise.

David made a decision that he would not forget God's Word no matter what was happening. He knew from past experiences that God's Word would quicken him. He said, *"I will never forget thy precepts: for with them thou hast quickened me. I am thine, save me; for I have sought thy precepts. The wicked have waited for me to destroy me: but I will consider thy testimonies"* (Psalm 119:93–95). When the enemy came to destroy him, David counted on the Lord. He focused on the promises in God's Word, even when people started standing in line to destroy him.

As the enemy waits to steal from you, bring destruction, and come in as a flood, what should you do? Consider God's testimonies. The psalmist said, *"My voice shalt thou hear in the morning, O LORD; in the morning will I direct my prayer unto thee, and will look up"* (Psalm 5:3). When trouble comes your way, praise God for His promises and remember His Word.

Trouble came to David and it will come to you, but you must focus on the promise and not the problem. As you praise God during difficulty, He will give you beauty for ashes, the oil of joy for mourning, and the garment of praise for the spirit of heaviness (Isaiah 61:3).

There is a great hymn that many dear Christians have been singing for years that goes:

> Some through the water, some through the flood,
> Some through the fire, but all through the blood;
> Some through great sorrow, but God gives a song.
> In the night season and all the day long.[2]

As Christians, we all go through the water and the fire. They are a part of life. There may be times when you will face moments when you think that the whole world is against you. In those moments, you must remember God's Word says, *"I will never leave thee, nor forsake thee"* (Hebrews 13:5).

Family members may leave someday. Friends come and go. It may seem as if you have lost everything. Perhaps you have already experienced these deep wounds. That is the day when you must go to the Lord and say, "Lord, Your Word says that You will preserve me." Or, "Lord, the enemy is after me to destroy me, but Your Word says that no evil will ever befall me." The key is that you must forget about your troubles, look past your wounds and scars, and begin to praise God. Those who make the choice to celebrate His faithful love, even when surrounded by disaster and hopelessness, are on the road to total recovery.

When the world forgets you, God does not. He will fulfill His Word in your life. Isaiah 55:11 says that God's Word will not return void, but *"it shall accomplish"* that which God pleases, and *"it shall prosper in the thing"* where God sent it.

A FINAL NOTE

Many times in our crusades we sing this jubilant song:

> When the Spirit of the Lord moves in my heart
> I will praise like David sang
>   I will praise
>   I will praise
> I will praise like David praised.[3]

The song celebrates trust in the Lord and establishing praise as a foundation for all times, good and bad. David recognized the importance of praise and laid a foundation in his life whereby he could stand securely upon the Rock—the name of the Lord Most High. Psalm 145:3 says, *"Great is the LORD, and greatly to be praised; and his greatness is unsearchable."*

Unsearchable? What a precious foundation! Deuteronomy 28:1–13 declares many of these unsearchable, unlimited promises upon which believers can build, including:

- God will set you on high above all the nations of the earth.
- You will be blessed in the city, and in the field.

- Your children will be blessed; your livestock will be blessed; your basket and store will be blessed.
- You will be blessed when you come in and when you go out.
- The Lord will shall cause your enemies that rise up against you to be smitten before you seven ways.
- The Lord will command blessings upon you in your storehouses, and in all that you set your hands to do.
- Your land will be blessed.
- The Lord will establish you holy unto Himself.
- God will make you the head, and not the tail.
- You will be above and not beneath.

As you obey the Word of the Lord and begin to honor Him with your praise, God will command blessings to overtake you. To overtake means that God's blessings will catch up with you, come upon you suddenly, and take you by surprise. God wants to bless you to the point that you are literally overwhelmed with His goodness and kept within His loving care.

The Lord is faithful to watch over His own. He came to this earth to win the battle for the lives of those who receive Him as Savior. Dwight L. Moody, the nineteenth-century evangelist, spoke of Jesus's victory by writing: "Jesus is the only man who ever conquered this world, the only complete victor. When he shouted on the cross, 'It is finished' (John 19:30), it was the shout of a conqueror. He had overcome every enemy."[4]

You, too, can begin moving into this fathomless dimension of victory. The transformation begins inside as you choose to honor and adore the Lord. Like David, you can recover all by building a foundation of praise in your life!

3

TOTAL RECOVERY
THROUGH PRAYER

Hear my prayer, O LORD, give ear to my supplications: in thy faithfulness answer me, and in thy righteousness.

—PSALM 143:1

Based upon what we read again and again through the Psalms, David learned how prayer is vital to anyone who desires safety, restoration, and abundance. He knew, through praying during the darkest hours, that supplication taps into God's faithfulness.

Only through prayer can we keep what God gives us. It is prayer that brings the anointing, and it is prayer that keeps the anointing. It is prayer that brings the miraculous; it is prayer that keeps the miraculous. Prayer brings deliverance, and prayer keeps us delivered.

There is mighty power in prayer. "Power" comes from the Greek word *exusia*, which means "delegated authority." The Lord Jesus has given you the right to stand in His stead and proclaim His victory in your situation and offer liberty to those ones who are captive.

Not only do you have His authority by promise, the Word of God also clearly declares that the devil has already been defeated. The Son of God, Jesus Christ, destroyed the works of the devil, and triumph is yours today.

Jesus won the victory and you have been given the privilege to enforce that victory, to administer that victory, to execute it, and to exercise it. The devil was given the spoil by Adam through sin, but today total recovery is yours by promise through Christ Jesus.

It is a precious privilege to demonstrate the victory of Christ! The Lord has left it up to us to administer His victory. The Holy Spirit actually aids you and me in enforcing Christ Jesus's victory in the earth; God causes us to triumph! He is the victorious One, and we are the triumphant ones.

Prayer Brings Recovery

Prayer enables you to enter a place that no demonic presence knows and the devil can not penetrate. Job 28:7-8 says, *"There is a path which no fowl knoweth, and which the vulture's eye hath not seen: The lion's whelps have not trodden it, nor the fierce lion passed by it."* The place of prayer is a place where you are completely covered and protected from harm.

In the secret place of prayer, you can put forth your hand *"upon the rock"*—meaning that you can touch God—and when you do *"he over-turneth the mountains by the roots"* (Job 28:9).   Mountains will be moved and rivers will begin to flow in your life when you pray: *"He cutteth out rivers among the rocks; and his eye seeth every precious thing"* (verse 10). Hidden things will also be revealed to you when prayer fills your life. Only God can move mountains, but prayer moves God.

James 5:16 declares, *"The effectual fervent prayer of a righteous man availeth much."* In R. A. Torrey's book *The Power of Prayer*, the evangelist wrote that he once knew a man who was an officer in a Sunday school in Brooklyn. One day the superintendent called on him to pray. He arose and said, "I am not a praying Christian; I am a working

Christian." Torrey commented on prayer as "the most effective work that anyone can do; that is, we can often bring more to pass by praying than we can by any other form of effort that we might put forth."[1]

Prayer is vital to your safekeeping and growth in Christ. As you call upon God, He will sustain you and bring complete restoration to your life.

My dear friend Dr. Oral Roberts once said to me, "If you want God to keep anointing you today and increase the anointing on you continually, you must pray as hard as you did when you had nothing."

David literally had next to nothing during those dark days in the cave as he began building a powerful nation from his unlikely 3-D army. Later, as his stature grew, he remained strong as long as he kept praying. It was through prayer that he moved into total recovery, as recorded in 1 Samuel 30:8: *"And David enquired at the LORD, saying, Shall I pursue after this troop? shall I overtake them? And he answered him, Pursue: for thou shalt surely overtake them, and without fail recover all."*

After all he had been through during the battles with Goliath, Saul, and the Amelekites, David was not inclined to act without prayerfully asking for God's direction. He showed, in full view of his army, that he was dependent upon God. David surrendered once again to the Lord's will.

In answer to his prayer, God not only confirmed what David was to do but also gave him the assurance of victory.

Prayer Keys

God was there when David faced wild animals as a shepherd boy. He was there when a youthful David stood in Goliath's massive shadow. He was there when David hid from Saul in the cave. God was there as David began leading his band of soldiers away from the prisons of distress, debt, and discontentment. David had built a lifelong relationship of prayer.

As with David, the Lord's will is to bring increase to you. He wants to bless, heal, and deliver. For that to happen, you must seek Him first. Here are simple keys to prayer that will help you stay focused on God's will for total recovery in your life:

1. Make sure your heart is praying, and you're not just speaking by rote. You do that by letting prayer flow from your innermost being, your heart. Let prayer be birthed within you before you speak it.

2. Do not be repetitious in prayer. Be specific with God when you pray and tell Him exactly what you need. *"Be not rash with thy mouth, and let not thine heart be hasty to utter any thing before God: for God is in heaven, and thou upon earth: therefore let thy words be few"* (Ecclesiastes 5:2).

3. Hide yourself in God and separate yourself from evil. Proverbs 27:12 says, *"A prudent man foreseeth the evil, and hideth himself; but the simple pass on, and are punished."* Prayer hides you in God's presence and disconnects you from the influence of this world.

When you pray, you are hid in Christ. No enemy can attack you. Prayer makes your life a succession of miracles. When you pray, you begin to inhale the atmosphere of heaven, and prayer itself becomes the breathing in of the Holy Ghost. Every time you pray, you exhale the world, and you inhale heaven. Prayer connects you with heaven and God's righteousness.

God's Will

God is looking for a people to pray His will to be done. Ezekiel 22:30 says, *"And I sought for a man among them, that should make up the hedge, and stand in the gap before me for the land, that I should not destroy it: but I found none."*

You see, prayer is not overcoming God's reluctance, but it is laying hold of His highest will. When you pray, you are not forcing God; instead, you are partnering with Him. Bring yourself into the will of God in prayer, find out what His plan for your life is by reading the Word and claiming His mighty promises, and then pray His promises over your life. As you hold His hand in prayer, He will lead you every step of the way.

Oftentimes when we pray, we want God to agree with us, but that is not prayer. John says in 1 John 5:14, *"And this is the confidence that we have in him, that, if we ask any thing according to his will, he heareth us."* The key to standing in agreement with God's will is knowing His promises and His Word.

Prayer is the language of the Holy Ghost, and it implements God's decisions. As you pray, you enter into a mighty partnership with God where you can stand on His promises and receive your victory.

The Day of Trouble

Have you ever felt like you were in a dark place that you just could not get out of? Has there ever been a time when you felt trapped by the enemy with nowhere to turn? In times of trouble, you can call upon the Lord and He will throw you the rope of the Holy Ghost and rescue you from the enemy. Nahum 1:7 says, *"The LORD is good, a strong hold in the day of trouble; and he knoweth them that trust in him."*

God wants to be there with you in the midst of your times of trouble as well. During those moments, you can call upon the Lord. Your Redeemer, Christ Jesus, is standing by to help when distress, worry, grief, affliction, pain, depression, entanglement, setbacks, sorrow, and loss come into your life. In fact, the word *redeemer* means "one who stands in your stead and buys back or pays a ransom for your sake." The Lord Jesus paid for your peace, healing, and restoration on the cross of Calvary. Atonement has already been made for your deliverance from sin and its consequences.

God hears the cry of those who are in trouble. David certainly remembered the Lord's ever-present help when he wrote, *"Call upon me in the day of trouble: I will deliver thee, and thou shalt glorify me"* (Psalm 50:15).

David had experienced God's faithfulness many times when he penned these words: *"For he hath looked down from the height of his sanctuary; from heaven did the LORD behold the earth; to hear the groaning of the prisoner; to loose those that are appointed to death"* (Psalm 102:19-20). He knew how God was faithful to hear the cry of His people and deliver them out of the bondage and slavery of Egypt.

Jeremiah the prophet also knew of God's faithfulness to both the children of Israel and to King David. Jeremiah is an example of a man who was in trouble and cried out to God. He said:

> *Mine enemies chased me sore, like a bird, without cause. They have cut off my life in the dungeon, and cast a stone upon me. Waters flowed over mine head; then I said, I am cut off. I called upon thy name, O LORD, out of the low dungeon. Thou hast heard my voice: hide not thine ear at my breathing, at my cry. Thou drewest near in the day that I called upon thee: thou saidst, Fear not. O LORD, thou hast pleaded the causes of my soul; thou hast redeemed my life.* (Lamentations 3:52–58)

The Lord will lead you in an abundant path as you seek Him. Jeremiah 31:9 declares, *"They shall come with weeping, and with supplications will I lead them: I will cause them to walk by the rivers of waters in a straight way, wherein they shall not stumble."*

As with Jeremiah, the enemy of your soul will try to make you feel like you are cut off from the rest of the world. Satan will plague your mind with condemnation and try to push thoughts of everything that is good and right out of your heart. Those are the times that, as you lift your voice to God in prayer, God will hear you from His holy hill and cause your enemies to scatter! Not a single prayer escapes your lips that the Lord does not hear. He is quick to deliver the one who calls upon Him in truth.

Strongholds that the devil has tried to place upon you must break away when you cry out to the mighty One of Israel in prayer. Prayer frees you from defeat and hopelessness and brings God's abundance and direction to your life.

What about the times when trouble hits so hard that you feel too weak to even pray? David knew about those, too. Psalm 40:12 describes some feelings that you may have experienced: *"For innumerable evils have compassed me about: mine iniquities have taken hold upon me, so that I am not able to look up; they are more than the hairs of mine head: therefore my heart faileth me."*

When you are unable to look up, never forget that the Lord is always watching over you. He knows your situation and where you are right now. The Lord is the strength of your heart. Psalm 73:26 says, *"My flesh and my heart faileth: but God is the strength of my heart and my portion for ever."*

Charles Finney once said these powerful truths:

> Every Christian has his season of being empty so that he may
> feel his dependence. However, soon he is clothed with

strength from on high, and an immortal, superhuman strength takes possession of his soul. The enemy gives way before him. In Christ he can run against a troop, and in His strength he can leap over a wall.[2]

The Lord will fill you with His supernatural strength from on high when you are too weak to pray. All that you have to do is mention His name. Just call upon the name of Jesus, and He will come near to you to help and strengthen you. The Lord looks at your heart, and He will be pleased to deliver you and will *"make haste to help"* you (Psalm 40:13).

Overcoming the Enemy

The moment you begin to pray and take your rightful place with God you will find Him mighty, right there by your side. Isaiah 12:6 says, *"Cry out and shout, thou inhabitant of Zion: for great is the Holy One of Israel in the midst of thee."*

Crying out to God implies seeking Him with all your heart: *"And ye shall seek me, and find me, when ye shall search for me with all your heart"* (Jeremiah 29:13). God promises to reveal Himself to you as you pray. He said, *"I will be found of you . . . and I will turn away your captivity"* (verse 14).

Prayer literally drives the devil away from all that belongs to you. The devil knows this and that is why he will fight to try to keep you from prayer. In Psalm 56:9, David proclaimed, *"When I cry unto thee, then shall mine enemies turn back: this I know; for God is for me."*

The devil flees when you pray and command him to go. The apostle Paul understood this revelation, and that is why he encouraged that we should *"pray without ceasing"* (Thessalonians 5:17).

The enemy knows he is defeated when you pray, so he will do

everything he can to keep you from prayer. That is why it is so important to make prayer a priority: set an appointment with God, and keep it!

As you make it a point to pray, things will come up that will interrupt and distract you. The phone may ring or someone may come to the door, but you must not allow these things to keep you from spending time with God.

You might even need to unplug your phone and ask your spouse or someone in your family to go and answer the door if someone knocks. Prayer is vital to every believer's life—it causes your very enemies to turn back—so whatever you do, do not miss time in fellowship with God.

Prayer Brings Restoration

Prayer is the key to your total recovery and restoration. As you pray, God washes your heart with the healing water of His presence. Fellowship with the Lord will make you whole. Remember the promises of total recovery found in Joel:

> And I will restore to you the years that the locust hath eaten, the cankerworm, and the caterpiller, and the palmerworm, my great army which I sent among you. And ye shall eat in plenty, and be satisfied, and praise the name of the LORD your God, that hath dealt wondrously with you: and my people shall never be ashamed. (Joel 2:25–26)

The promise of restoration is tied to the principle of prayer. In fact, three times the Lord said to "pray" in Joel 2 before He promised to restore the years, to pour out His Spirit's blessing on the people, and to drive out the enemy.

The message here is very clear: God will empower you and destroy the works of the enemy when you pray. The Lord Jesus will bind the devil, who has tried to bind you, attack you, and steal what belongs to you, as you call upon Jesus's holy name in prayer.

Your prayer is the vehicle that God Almighty flows through to accomplish His purpose and will in the earth. When you speak and say, "In the name of Jesus," God flows through your words and flows through your life as a channel for His power. That is the reason you can command the enemy to go with boldness. Jesus has all authority and He gave it to you.

Through prayer, God releases His mighty power to open prison doors and set captives free. Prayer changes us and changes things as He begins moving when you stand upon His name.

THREE WORLDS OF PRAYER

Matthew 7:7-8 says, *"Ask, and it shall be given you; seek, and ye shall find; knock, and it shall be opened unto you: For every one that asketh receiveth; and he that seeketh findeth; and to him that knocketh it shall be opened."* There are three worlds of prayer: the world of asking, the world of seeking, and the world of knocking.

1. Asking. The world of asking is the first step that you take in prayer, and it deals with your desires and longings. This world is the place where you make your requests known to God. It is the place where you pour out your heart to Him and tell Him exactly what you need.

2. Seeking. The world of seeking is the second step, and it deals with the presence of God. It is the place where you seek His divine presence in your life. Hebrews 11:6 says, *"But without faith it is impossible to please him: for he that cometh to God must believe that he is, and* *that he is a rewarder of them that diligently seek him."* When you seek God diligently, you may say as David did, *"As the hart panteth after the water brooks, so panteth my soul after thee, O God"* (Psalm 42:1). Seeking is the place of hungering for His presence.

3. Knocking. The world of knocking is the third step to take in prayer; it deals with intercession. Intercession happens when you, through prayer, put yourself in the place of another. As you intercede for another, you offer them your support or help in prayer, pleading on their behalf to the Father. The Lord Jesus intercedes for you as your Mediator. Romans 8:34 says, *"It is Christ that died, yea rather, that is risen again, who is even at the right hand of God, who also maketh intercession for us."*

Asking deals with your needs, seeking deals with God's presence and God's desires, and knocking deals with the needs of another person.

As you wait upon the Lord, He will help you to pray, enabling you to call upon His mighty name. God will fill you with power in prayer so you can claim His promises of recovery as you ask, seek, and knock.

Andrew Murray, a prolific writer whose books have stirred men to the depth of their souls asked:

> Who will yield himself, like Paul, to be an intercessor? Who will plead not only with but also for the believers around him, that they may learn to expect the almighty power of God to work in them? What has previously appeared beyond their reach may become the object of their longing desire and their confident assurance: a life of faith in which Christ reigns in their hearts.[3]

God will use you mightily when you ask, seek, and knock. Call upon His name. Every enemy will flee from before you as you walk in fellowship with the Lord. God will, through you, set others free and fill them with the same great faith, which you, too, stand upon as you pray.

Prayer of Agreement

Prayer has special power when you pray in agreement with others. Matthew 18:19 declares, *"If two of you shall agree on earth as touching any thing that they shall ask, it shall be done for them of my Father which is in heaven."*

What is the prayer of agreement and why is it so vital to total recovery?

The prayer of agreement is standing in one accord, in mutual faith and understanding with another person, for a specific prayer request or need. The prayer of agreement is vital because there are times when you simply cannot pray through to victory on your own. The prayer of agreement enables you to press through to a certain victory in Christ. The Bible is filled with amazing examples of the power available through agreement.

The story of Joshua fighting against Amalek is one. Moses, Aaron, and Hur prayed together for victory. Exodus 17:8-9 says, *"Then came Amalek, and fought with Israel in Rephidim. And Moses said unto Joshua, Choose us out men, and go out, fight with Amalek: to morrow I will stand on the top of the hill with the rod of God in mine hand."* These warriors stood together, asking for God's help as they stood against the evil Amalek.

You undoubtedly have already faced many "Amaleks." There will be many evil forces in the future. Ephesians 6:12 says, *"For we wrestle not against flesh and blood, but against principalities, against powers, against the rulers of the darkness of this world, against spiritual wickedness in high places."*

There are times in our lives, just like with Joshua, when we need to join our faith with that of others to break through strongholds. Moses told Joshua that he would stand on the top of the hill. Standing is a powerful symbol. Ephesians 6:14 says, *"Stand therefore, having your loins girt about with truth, and having on the breastplate of righteousness."* Standing symbolizes working, while sitting symbolizes resting.

Moses said that he would stand on top of the hill. He was telling Joshua to go fight and that while Joshua was fighting, he would stand in agreement for victory with him. Exodus 17:10 tells us that *"Joshua did as Moses had said to him, and fought with Amalek: and Moses, Aaron, and Hur went up to the top of the hill."*

Moses asked Aaron and Hur to agree with him. God honors the power of agreement throughout the Old and New Testaments. As a result, *"And it came to pass, when Moses held up his hand, that Israel prevailed: and when he let down his hand, Amalek prevailed"* (Exodus 17:11).

Agreement brought victory to Joshua against the Amalekites, and agreement in prayer will bring victory in your life against your enemies. You cannot have success against the enemy if you are sitting. You must stand strong in prayer.

Spiritual battle in prayer against the enemy can drain your strength and make you weary. When fatigue sets in, it becomes difficult to pray correctly. That is when you need someone's help to stand with you and support you, assisting you as you pray.

Exodus 17:12 says, *"But Moses' hands were heavy; and they took a stone, and put it under him, and he sat thereon; and Aaron and Hur stayed up his hands, the one on the one side, and the other on the other side; and his hands were steady until the going down of the sun."*

The power of agreement enabled Joshua to have victory over Amalek *"with the edge of the sword"* (verse 13). Hebrews also tells us that the Word of God is quick, powerful, and sharper than *"any twoedged sword, piercing even to the dividing asunder of soul and spirit, and of the joints and marrow, and is a discerner of the thoughts and intents of the heart"* (Hebrews 4:12).

The Word of God upon your lips is a mighty weapon against your enemy, and your enemies will be defeated, just as the enemies of the Lord's people throughout the Old and New Testaments were defeated when His people stood together in agreement.

Agree with Whom?

If agreement in prayer is essential to overcoming certain battles, whom should you call to stand with you?

It is important that you pray with someone who is likeminded, one whose heart is with you. In other words, you must stand in prayer with someone who is connected with you spiritually. The apostle Paul said: *"And we beseech you, brethren, to know them which labour among you"* (1 Thessalonians 5:12).

Moses understood the power of unity in prayer, and that is why he only had those who were close to him (Aaron and Hur) praying with him. Aaron was Moses's brother and Hur was one of Moses's leaders. Scripture tells us that Hur was Caleb's son (Caleb was one of Moses's generals): *"And when Azubah was dead, Caleb took unto him Ephrath, which bare him Hur. And Hur begat Uri, and Uri begat Bezaleel"* (1 Chronicles 2:19–20). Bezaleel was the man God anointed to help Moses build the Tabernacle, and he was Hur's grandson. Hur's whole family was involved in the ministry with Moses.

Eleazar, the priest, also understood the importance of knowing and praying the will of God. In the book of Numbers, Moses brought Joshua to Eleazar as the Lord commanded so that a man could be set over the congregation to lead them. Numbers 27:21 says, *"And he shall stand before Eleazar the priest, who shall ask counsel for him after the judgment of Urim before the* LORD.*"*

David understood the principle that agreement with likeminded believers was essential to recovering all that was stolen from him. In 1 Samuel 30, before David ever went into battle, he sought Abiathar, the high priest, to bring the ephod with the urim and thummim so he would know whether to go into battle or not.

In the Old Testament, before the birth of Jesus when God walked and spoke with men, He used various channels of communication with His people. One of those channels was the ephod, which contained the urim and thummim: two black and white stones which spoke of light and perfection in Hebrew. The high priest carried the urim and thummim in the pouch of his breastplate. Exodus 28 speaks of the ephod as being a part of the priest's garment so that "*he may minister*" to God in the priest's office (verse 4). Some scholars believe that the stones would brighten or grow dim according to God's will and whether it was yes or no.

These stones were symbolic of the revelation of the Spirit. The Holy Spirit was not poured out in Israel in that day as He has been since Pentecost. For the most part, men knew the voice of God through the prophets as God spoke to them. That is why the prophets were needed to come and say, "Thus saith the Lord."

Abiathar was called to bring the ephod so he could help David seek God's counsel. David sought the urim and thummim to help him know if he should go into battle or not. If the stones brightened, David knew that meant yes, and if the stones grew dim, David knew he should not go.

David's decision to seek Abiathar for agreement and the will of God through the ephod clearly said, "I am coming into the presence of God, and I will not come out until God answers me. I am going to seek Him until I find Him."

There is a mighty revelation in this story: If David had not needed Abiathar, he would not have called for him. David sought the will of God in the power of agreement knowing that it was vital to his success in recovering all.

As God's people, we should seek for His will to be close to our hearts. Aaron did just that as he ministered before the Lord, wearing the ephod. Exodus 28:30 says that Aaron had them *"upon his heart before the LORD continually."*

The Bible, describing David as *"a man after [God's] own heart"* (Acts 13:22), shows that David diligently sought God's will and presence. It says in 2 Samuel 6:14 that as he wore the ephod, he *"danced before the LORD with all of his might."*

David was given great authority as he sought God's will. Wrote Watchman Nee, a powerful man of God who was imprisoned for his faith:

> All who are used by God to be in authority must have the spirit of David. Let no one defend himself nor speak for himself. Learn to wait and to be humble before God. He who knows how to obey best is he who is best qualified to be in authority. The lower one prostrates himself before God the quicker the Lord will vindicate him.[4]

Moses, Joshua, and David all knew the importance of praying only with those who were connected with them in the spirit. It is most important that you follow their biblical example and never take a stranger to pray the prayer of agreement with you. In order for agreement in prayer to be effective, you must pray with someone who has a like heart with you.

Determine in your heart today to pursue God as passionately as David did. As you press into His presence by standing in the prayer of agreement, He will reveal His will to you and grant you mighty authority.

God in the Midst of Agreement

God Almighty has given you and me power in prayer, saying, *"If two of you shall agree…it shall be done"* (Matthew 18:19). The Word is clear that whatsoever you bind on earth will be bound in heaven and whatsoever you loose on earth will be loosed in heaven. You cannot bind and loose by yourself; the Lord must be in the midst of you. Binding and loosing always happens in agreement, and never without it.

As God's children, we must never underestimate the power of agreement. It is easy to neglect this truth and go into prayer by yourself for days and even for years, praying for the same thing, yet nothing happens. At that point many give up, thinking that God did not hear them, when in truth we must realize that certain types of prayers demand agreement.

Jesus in the Garden of Gethsemane looked for someone to tarry with Him in prayer:

> *Then cometh Jesus with them unto a place called Gethsemane, and saith unto the disciples, Sit ye here, while I go and pray yonder. And he took with him Peter and the two sons of Zebedee, and began to be sorrowful and very heavy. Then saith he unto them, My soul is exceeding sorrowful, even unto death: tarry ye here, and watch with me.* (Matthew 26:36–38)

Jesus requested Peter to pray with Him because Peter was the closest to Him in spirit at that time. John was closer to Jesus later on, but Peter was the closest to Jesus when He prayed in the garden.

Sadly, though, Peter was asleep instead of praying. Matthew 26:40–41 says, *"And he cometh unto the disciples, and findeth them asleep, and saith unto Peter, What, could ye not watch with me one hour? Watch and pray, that ye enter not into temptation: the spirit indeed is willing, but the flesh is weak."*

If the Son of God knew that He needed agreement in prayer, how much more do you and I need to realize the same? Christ needed the prayer of agreement in the Garden of Gethsemane. There will be times when you will need the prayer of agreement, too.

God in heaven is released into action through agreement in prayer on earth. Matthew 6:9–10 says, *"After this manner therefore pray ye,"* and then Jesus showed us the prayer of agreement, saying, *"Thy kingdom come. Thy will be done in earth, as it is in heaven."* Jesus told us to come into agreement and pray for God's will. As we are faithful to gather in His name, He will be in the midst of us.

Strength in Numbers

The prayer of agreement brings a powerful increase to your prayers. Deuteronomy 32:30 says, *"How should one chase a thousand, and two put ten thousand to flight, except their Rock had sold them, and the LORD had shut them up?"* There are times we need to agree with someone to see the tenfold increase in power. You may experience times when you cannot break through, and the battle has made you weary. When that becomes the case, you will need someone to help you pray. If Moses, Joshua, David, and even Jesus needed agreement, how much more do we?

When you experience loss in your life, you will need someone to stand with you and support you, and the best person you can count on is your spouse or a family member or a dear friend who is connected with you in the Holy Ghost. The Lord places special individuals in your life to pray the prayer of faith with you, and His Word promises that when you agree together, it will put your enemies to flight.

All throughout the Word of God, you will see the prayer of agreement. Jonathan agreed with David. Aaron and Hur agreed with Moses. Silas agreed with Paul in prison. Jesus looked for Peter to pray with Him in the Garden of Gethsemane.

When you agree in prayer, God, will open doors to you that you thought were closed. Acts 16:25–26 says, *"And at midnight Paul and Silas prayed, and sang praises unto God: and the prisoners heard them. And suddenly there was a great earthquake, so that the foundations of the prison were shaken: and immediately all the doors were opened, and every one's bands were loosed."* As Paul and Silas agreed in prayer, the Lord moved suddenly to set them free. The Scripture states that *"all the doors were opened."* When you call upon the Lord, He will make a way for you when there seems to be no way.

Another story of the power of agreement is found in Acts 12:5: *"Peter therefore was kept in prison: but prayer was made without ceasing of the church unto God for him."* As you continue to read that story, you see that the angel of God came to the prison, opened the doors, loosed Peter, and showed Peter the way out because the church prayed. During those days, the church met in a house, and probably no more than twenty people prayed in agreement together. God heard and miraculously answered their prayers, and Peter was set free.

Peter did not know where he was going when the angel told him to put his sandals on, but he followed, and the next thing he knew, he was outside and free. God will do the same for you if you will stand in the prayer of agreement with someone today. You can see your son, daughter, family member, or friend set free.

Ten Results from Agreement

Many marvelous benefits can come to your life as you stand in the prayer of agreement, but here are ten headlines that will mightily affect you.

1. The prayer of agreement will bring victory to your life. Exodus 17:12 says, *"But Moses' hands were heavy; and they took a stone, and put it under him, and he sat thereon; and Aaron and Hur stayed up his hands."* Victory comes through agreement. In agreement, whatsoever you bind will be bound; whatsoever you loose will be loosed.

2. The prayer of agreement will provide you a way of escape. God's Word promises that He will make a way of escape: *"There hath no temptation taken you but such as is common to man: but God is faithful, who will not suffer you to be tempted above that ye are able; but will with the temptation also make a way to escape, that ye may be able to bear it"* (1 Corinthians 10:13).

3. The prayer of agreement enables you to make the right decisions. In Acts 1:14, the apostles and disciples agreed in prayer regarding two men who were appointed (with one to be chosen) to replace Judas as an apostle and a witness. The Word of God says, *"These all continued with one accord in prayer and supplication, with the women, and Mary the mother of Jesus, and with his brethren."*

As the apostles prayed, they waited upon the Lord for the right decision about the men. Acts 1:24 says, *"And they prayed, and said, Thou, Lord, which knowest the hearts of all men, shew whether of these two thou hast chosen."* Through the prayer of agreement, God gave them direction on whom to appoint. Just as agreement in prayer helped Jesus's disciples, it can help you.

4. The prayer of agreement will bring the Holy Ghost in His fullness and power upon your life. Acts 2:1–2 says, *"And when the day* *of Pentecost was fully come, they were all with one accord in one place. And suddenly there came a sound from heaven as of a rushing mighty wind, and it filled all the house where they were sitting."* Jesus and His disciples were gathered in one accord and in one place; that is total agreement. When you enter into agreement, God will fill you with power and move in your life, too. Great revivals of the past, such as the Welsh Revival, the Great Awakening, and the Azusa Street Outpouring began because of prayer in agreement. As you read the histories of these revivals, you find that people joined in prayer, seeking God until His power fell. God will do the same for you, filling you with the Spirit if you will join with others and pray.

5. **The prayer of agreement will bring miracles into your life**. Peter and John went to the temple together, and in the power of the name of Jesus, they saw a lame man healed. Acts 3:6 says, *"Silver and gold have I none; but such as I have give I thee: In the name of Jesus Christ of Nazareth rise up and walk."* When you join your faith with another in prayer, the miraculous happens as a result.

6. **The prayer of agreement brings great power and grace.** Acts 4:31–33 says, *"And when they had prayed, the place was shaken where they were assembled together; and they were all filled with the Holy Ghost, and they spake the word of God with boldness. And the multitude of them that believed were of one heart and of one soul: neither said any of them that ought of the things which he possessed was his own; but they had all things common. And with great power gave the apostles witness of the resurrection of the Lord Jesus: and great grace was upon them all."* Great power and grace will come upon your life as you agree in prayer.

7. **The prayer of agreement brings abundance to you and your home.** Acts 4:34–35 says, *"Neither was there any among them that lacked: for as many as were possessors of lands or houses sold them, and brought the prices of the things that were sold, And laid them down at the*

apostles' feet: and distribution was made unto every man according as he had need." There was no lack among them because of their agreement. Agreement brings abundance.

8. The prayer of agreement brings freedom from bondage. In the book of Acts, Peter was led out of prison by an angel as God's people prayed together. As you pray in agreement, bondages that have kept you back and slowed you down will fall away. Some people today are not in a natural prison but a spiritual prison. You may know someone who is in this state and needs to be set free. If you will agree in prayer with another, God will bring liberty and freedom to their life.

9. The prayer of agreement will bring you boldness for ministry. Ephesians 6:18–20 says, *"Praying always with all prayer and supplication in the Spirit, and watching thereunto with all perseverance and supplication for all saints; And for me, that utterance may be given unto me, that I may open my mouth boldly, to make known the mystery of the gospel, For which I am an ambassador in bonds: that therein I may speak boldly, as I ought to speak."* As you pray in agreement, fire from heaven will fill your soul and mighty boldness will come over you to proclaim the message of Jesus Christ.

10. The prayer of agreement brings the Word of God into places closed to the Word of God. Paul said, *"Finally, brethren, pray for us, that the word of the Lord may have free course, and be glorified, even as it is with you: And that we may be delivered from unreasonable and wicked men: for all men have not faith"* (2 Thessalonians 3:1–2). Power falls when liberty is given to allow the Gospel to be presented freely. It was because of the prayer of agreement that God opened the doors to Russia, and it will be because of agreement that God will send His Word into other countries still closed to the Gospel. Colossians 4:2–3 says, *"Continue in prayer, and watch in the same with thanksgiving; Withal praying also for us, that God would open unto us a door of utter-*

ance, to speak the mystery of Christ, for which I am also in bonds." The same truth that applies to God's Word going forth into nations that were once closed to it also applied to families and homes that are closed to it. You may know a family like this who does not want the Word of God in their home, nor do they want to hear about the Gospel. The prayer of agreement opens doors. God will give you the opportunity to share with them when you pray.

PRIVILEGE AND POWER OF AGREEMENT

The prayer of agreement is a privilege and a power that is available to you as a believer in the Lord Jesus. Those who do not pray are lacking much in God. Prayer brings you into the realm of the divine where God Almighty is. Prayer moves you from earth to heaven where you exhale self and inhale the infilling of the Holy Spirit.

If prayer brings such power to the believer's life, why are so many Christians lacking in prayer? The answer is simple: when you do not pray, you serve the flesh. It is vital to your recovery that you serve God and not self. Recovery will not begin in your life until you praise and pray.

The power of agreement in prayer is the key to your success, just as it was for Moses, Joshua, David, and Jesus Christ. God's will is to bring increase to you, but He will not do it until you ask Him. James 4:2 is a reminder: *"Ye have not, because ye ask not."* You must go to the Lord in prayer and ask Him to bring your answer.

Wrote Smith Wigglesworth, a man whom God flowed through with powerful signs and wonders:

> Being more than overcomers is to have a shout at the end of
> the fight. It not only means overcoming, but it also means

being able to stand when we have overcome and not fall down. I count it a great privilege that God has opened my eyes to see that His great plan has been arranged for us before the foundation of the world, and we may all just come into line with God to believe that these things that He has promised must come to pass to whoever believes.[5]

Those who believe must stand in agreement, knowing that they have overcome. The will of God is governed by the prayers of the saints. God wills it, we agree to it, and then heaven performs it.

A FINAL WORD

Sometimes one prayer will not do. Sometimes two days of prayer will not do. God knows that you are serious about seeking Him when you pray, keep praying, and never give up. When God sees your determination, especially as you come into agreement with others of the same heart, He will even send angels to bring your answer. In prison, the angel of the Lord came to Peter and *"a light shined in the prison: and he smote Peter on the side, and raised him up, saying, Arise up quickly. And his chains fell off from his hands"* (Acts 12:7). Not only was Peter released from prison because of prayer, but Herod, who had imprisoned Peter, was slain. God will destroy your enemies if you will pray.

When the enemy comes against you, you can pull down strongholds through prayer. You can stand against him with the Word of God, a twoedged sword in your hand, and say, "No, in Jesus's name!" Prayer penetrates the enemy's camp, delivers captives, and releases the spoils that have been stolen from you.

Daniel prayed twenty-one days before he got his answer, and you may need to pray for a season too. But never forget that breakthrough will come to you as you are committed to pray. Luke 18:7–8 says, *"And shall not God avenge his own elect, which cry day and night unto him, though he bear long with them? I tell you that he will avenge them speedily."*

God's direction and promise for you today is to pray for total recovery, *"for thou shalt surely overtake them, and without fail recover all"* (1 Samuel 30:8). Prayer will help you prevail against your enemies. Everything begins changing when you tap into the power of prayer.

4

TOTAL RECOVERY
THROUGH PURSUIT

◆◆◆

Pursue after your enemies . . . for the LORD your God hath delivered them into your hand.

—JOSHUA 10:19

What is pursuit, in a spiritual sense? More importantly, what does pursuing the enemy have to do with our total recovery?

David received a clear word from the Lord regarding pursuing his enemy: *"And David enquired at the LORD, saying, Shall I pursue after this troop? shall I overtake them? And he answered him, Pursue: for thou shalt surely overtake them, and without fail recover all"* (1 Samuel 30:8).

As David pursued his enemy, he recovered all. You can, too, as you pursue your enemies. Spiritual pursuit takes place when you put your prayer into action by moving upon what you believe in. David prayed and then he acted in faith. In Aramaic, the word for faith is *faithing*, which means "faith that is acting." David prayed and then he acted. Faith acts, and faith is not faith unless it is moving and living faith.

Hebrews 11:1 says, *"Now faith is the substance of things hoped for, the evidence of things not seen."* This passage begins with "now faith," revealing that faith is present tense. Faith is always in the now. It is always in the present, and if it is not now, it is not faith.

David pursued his enemies by acting upon what God said to him. The Lord said to pursue, so David acted upon God's command: *"So David went, he and the six hundred men that were with him"* (1 Samuel 30:9). David put his faith into action by following through with what God had spoken for Him to do. He did not sit idly, hoping for something to happen. He pursued his enemy, and God gave him the victory.

ACTING ON FAITH

The Bible calls the devil a thief, one who steals. Thieves do not just walk around looking at things. Neither do they usually bother to take low-end goods. No! They steal things that are valuable to you.

John 10:10 paints a clear picture of this: *"The thief cometh not, but for to steal, and to kill, and to destroy: I am come that they might have life, and that they might have it more abundantly."*

God is a giver, and Satan is a taker. God restores, and Satan steals. God recovers, and Satan removes. In fact, God gives so much life that it is not just life; it is abundant life, or life that is so great that it flows out of you to touch others. Abundant life can be described as a cup that runs over with life, so much so that you have to drink from your saucer because your cup is overflowing.

David experienced the loss of a thief and the goodness of God's promises. It says in 1 Samuel 30:10: *"David pursued."* He sought out the enemy and persisted in following God's word. Many Christians do not know how to pursue, and they become fearful at the thought of going into battle. God girds His people with *"strength unto the battle,"* and He will subdue those who rise up against you (Psalm 18:39).

In order to recover all, you must be willing to put your faith in God's

Word as David did and pursue your enemy. It is up to you to aggressively go after everything that God promised to give you in His Word.

The deeper you go in the Spirit, the more you find out that you're still on the surface. God wants you to reach great depth in Him. Psalm 42:7 says, *"Deep calleth unto deep at the noise of thy waterspouts."* There is a place, in the Spirit, where your very being cries out to the Lord in prayer, but you cannot know that place if you do not pursue God's promises with intensity.

Every miracle that took place in God's Word happened with action on the part of the individual who was in need.

Exodus 14:15–16 says, *"And the LORD said unto Moses, Wherefore criest thou unto me? speak unto the children of Israel, that they go forward: But lift thou up thy rod, and stretch out thine hand over the sea, and divide it: and the children of Israel shall go on dry ground through the midst of the sea."*

God asked Moses, "Why are you still crying to me?" Then the Lord told him to "speak" or act upon his faith in Him. God told Moses to lift up the rod, stretch his hand out over the sea, and go forth. Moses's instruction from the Lord was to march on and keep going. As he did, the Red Sea split before him. Moses witnessed the miraculous as he acted upon his faith in God.

Then God gave the Israelites the Promised Land to possess: *"And the LORD said unto me, Behold, I have begun to give Sihon and his land before thee: begin to possess, that thou mayest inherit his land"* (Deuteronomy 2:31). God said, *"I have begun to give."* He doesn't give until people start moving and acting upon faith. He will take care of the enemy in your way, but once He gives you the land, you must go and possess it. He often leaves it up to you to overcome the obstacles. Most importantly, you cannot inherit something until you take ownership—until you receive what God has promised you.

Move forward into the New Testament. Think about the faith that it took for Bartimaeus to cry out to the Lord, *"Have mercy on me"* (Mark 10:47). Those around him were most likely discomforted by his yelling, and they may have even told him to be quiet. Nevertheless, he kept shouting out, *"Lord, have mercy on me, Son of David, have mercy on me"* (verse 48). Bartemaeus was acting upon his faith. The result—he got his answer!

We find the same scenario in the story of the woman with the issue of blood. She also acted upon her faith when she said, *"If I may but touch his clothes, I shall be whole"* (Mark 5:28). She reached out for her answer, the Lord Jesus, and He healed her.

The early church is another example of faith in action. On the Day of Pentecost, *"They were all filled with the Holy Ghost, and began to speak with other tongues, as the Spirit gave them utterance"* (Acts 2:4). Believers prayed and then began to speak, acting upon the revelation and infilling that God had given them. As with the early church, we must not wait and then react, but rather we must act first in faith and then see God move. You see, pursuit is faith in action: *"Without faith it is impossible to please him: for he that cometh to God must believe that he is, and that he is a rewarder of them that diligently seek him"* (Hebrews 11:6). Pursuit, active faith, brings victory!

The more you come to know the Lord, the more you find out that He has so much more waiting for you to receive, yet nothing miraculous happens without faith. Until Moses stretched the rod over the Red Sea, the water stayed intact. Until the children of Israel were ready to possess the Promised Land, they wandered forty years in the wilderness. Until David unleashed the small stone from his sling, Goliath towered over him, sneering at the young man's God. Until Bartimaeus and the woman with the issue of blood acted in faith, their miracle remained unfulfilled.

This is true even of salvation. Forgiveness is a free gift, bought by the death, burial, and resurrection of Jesus Christ. Yet God does not force you to accept the Savior into your heart. You can do that only of your own free will.

Pursuit is the key!

Belief in Action

After Jesus's resurrection, Jesus told Thomas, *"Reach hither thy finger, and behold my hands; and reach hither thy hand, and thrust it into my side: and be not faithless, but believing"* (John 20:27). Thomas had trouble believing that it could truly be Jesus, resurrected and standing before him. When Thomas touched the Lord, he was astonished by the physical proof that he beheld, *"Thomas answered and said unto him, My Lord and my God"* (verse 28).

Jesus went on to encourage, *"Thomas, because thou hast seen me, thou hast believed: blessed are they that have not seen, and yet have believed"* (verse 29). You receive a special blessing as God's child when you believe in faith.

The Lord Jesus was very patient with Thomas and helped him to see the reality of his faith. The minute God sees your faith, He will move on your behalf. All you must do is act upon your faith because *"as the body without the spirit is dead, so faith without works is dead also"* (James 2:26).

God will reveal His will to you as you are moving. Abraham's servant Eliezer remains a powerful example. God showed Eliezer the way while he was moving. Genesis 24:27 says, *"I being in the way, the LORD led me to the house of my master's brethren."* Pursuit is best accomplished while moving.

Active Faith

Pursuit requires faith. And faith is acting upon what you believe in God, despite the circumstances: *"For we walk by faith, not by sight"*

(2 Corinthians 5:7). Faith believes Him, not just in words alone, but also in deed. If faith is not acting and alive, it is not faith.

Luke 16:16 says, *"The law and the prophets were until John: since that time the kingdom of God is preached, and every man presseth into it."* You press into God's kingdom by taking hold of the promises of God by faith. And by understanding this principle, you take a major step forward toward your own total recovery.

Did you know that you could embrace the promises of God? I love what Hebrews 11:13 tells us: *"These all died in faith, not having received the promises, but having seen them afar off, and were persuaded of them, and embraced them, and confessed that they were strangers and pilgrims on the earth."* This passage from the "faith chapter" means you can actually take God's promises and press them close to your heart so they will never escape you.

As you combine your faith with works, you will begin to see God's promises come to pass, for faith always has a destination. Faith pursues! Faith involves going somewhere as you put your whole heart into believing the precious promises in God's Word.

Romans 10:10 declares, *"For with the heart man believeth unto righteousness; and with the mouth confession is made unto salvation."* That is moving faith with a destination. That is faith that is born in the heart and coming out of the life. Faith then moves out of the life and has a destination. Faith never stays locked up inside. It goes from your heart to your mouth (or speech), and then it reveals itself in all areas of your life.

PURSUIT DESPITE OBSTACLES

With great faith David was confident in his heart that God would be his help as he fought against his enemies. He said, *"For by thee I have run through a troop; and by my God have I leaped over a wall"* (Psalm 18:29).

He counted on the Lord to be his Rock and said that the Lord teaches his hands to war with great strength.

The enemy builds walls to try and prevent you from getting to where God wants you to go, but if the devil puts a wall in front of you, you can leap over it as David did. You can trust the Lord to make your steps sure. Psalm 18:36–37 says, *"Thou hast enlarged my steps under me, that my feet did not slip. I have pursued mine enemies, and overtaken them: neither did I turn again till they were consumed."*

One wall is relying on reason instead of walking by faith. What is reason? It is trying to figure things out in your own understanding. I once heard someone say, "God said it, I believe it, and that settles it." There is no reason—just belief. You must simply decide to believe what God said, no matter what comes your way.

Reason is good in its right place and in its right realm. You need good reasoning in the natural; otherwise, you would not be living properly on earth. However, reason does not have an important place in the spirit realm. In the spirit realm, you simply believe.

As you believe, the power of God upon your life will enable you to pursue your enemy and overtake him. Psalm 18:38–39 says, *"I have wounded them that they were not able to rise: they are fallen under my feet. For thou hast girded me with strength unto the battle: thou hast subdued under me those that rose up against me."*

There will be times in your walk with God that obstacles stand in your way. God will not move every obstacle. He leaves some of them up for you to overcome, however He specifically equips you with all you need to make your individual journey.

God told the children of Israel, *"Rise ye up, take your journey"* (Deuteronomy 2:24). God commanded them to get on their feet and prepare to expand, broaden, and increase. Then the Lord told them to *"pass over the river Arnon."* They knew they had a river to cross, or an obstacle to overcome, on their way. Unlike the Jordan River and the Red Sea, God did not promise that He would divide the Arnon River. Instead, he told them to cross over it. Three million people needed to pass over the river, and God left it up to them to overcome that obstacle.

It is no different today. You must rise up if you want to overcome your obstacles.

Go back to the example of Noah. God allowed his servant to overcome many obstacles. God provided deliverance from destruction for Noah, but first Noah had to build the ark. Noah acted upon his faith, and God led him through each challenge. God's promise for Noah was, *"Behold, I establish my covenant with you, and with your seed after you"* (Genesis 9:9).

God will establish you in His kingdom—just as He did for the children of Israel and Noah—as you stand upon His Word, act upon your faith, and refuse to be stopped or slowed.

Hebrews 12:1 speaks of this determination: *"Let us lay aside every weight, and the sin which doth so easily beset us, and let us run with patience the race that is set before us."* Even a novice runner knows that heavy, unnecessary clothing slows you down, often keeping you from pursuing the goal. Sin is the same way; it slows you down. In order to run the race and win in this Christian life, you must follow the instructions found in Proverbs 4:26–27: *"Ponder the path of thy feet, and let all thy ways be established. Turn not to the right hand nor to the left: remove thy foot from evil."*

Don't let any obstacle, opposition, or temptation keep you from pursuing total recovery!

PURSUIT DESPITE AVOIDANCE AND INACTION

Moving forward cannot happen in a world of inaction. Slothfulness is a deadly sin to fall into. Those who are spiritually inactive cannot obtain what belongs to them. The Word of God gives many references to this state which reveal a clear picture of the hindrance to faithful pursuit.

Proverbs 26:13 describes a man who is fearful to move out because of the enemy, *"The slothful man saith, There is a lion in the way; a lion is in the streets."* Some individuals say, "The devil is out there," and they fear that if they try to do anything he will come after them. You must not live in fear, but in faith. It is important that you get this into your spirit, because slothfulness is a disease that will devastate your life if you allow it to.

Proverbs 12:24 declares, *"The hand of the diligent shall bear rule: but the slothful shall be under tribute."* In other words, the negligent individual is always in bondage.

Likewise, Proverbs 15:19 states, *"The way of the slothful man is as an hedge of thorns: but the way of the righteous is made plain."* In other words, the person who is lax and listless is walking in a cursed land with cursed ground.

Look at Proverbs 18:9: *"He also that is slothful in his work is brother to him that is a great waster."* The idle person is equal to the one who carelessly wastes what God gives him.

Examine Ecclesiastes 10:18: *"By much slothfulness the building decayeth; and through idleness of the hands the house droppeth through."* Whatever a slothful man builds will collapse.

Inactive people don't seem to enjoy life. Solomon experienced this and said in Ecclesiastes 2:17: *"Therefore I hated life; because the work that is wrought under the sun is grievous unto me: for all is vanity and vexation of spirit."*

Granted, there have been times when every believer experiences dry spells and weariness, but slothfulness and inactivity should never be allowed to enter. It is vital that you remain passionate about knowing God and standing on His Word.

Wrote Madam Jeanne Guyon, a cherished sixteenth-century writer,

"Yours is a God who often hides Himself. He hides Himself for a purpose. Why? His purpose is to rouse you from spiritual laziness."[1]

When you are tempted to allow spiritual laziness to harm your pursuit of all God has given you to recover, resist the temptation. Arise and possess the land that has been given to you. Judges 18:9 says, *"Arise, that we may go up against them: for we have seen the land, and, behold, it is very good: and are ye still? be not slothful to go, and to enter to possess the land."* As you guard against spiritual laziness, you will arise to go and get what God has promised you.

Pursuit as a Soldier

Not only should you pursue as a relentless runner, you should remember that you are a soldier: *"Thou therefore endure hardness, as a good soldier of Jesus Christ"* (2 Timothy 2:3). As a warrior in God's army, you are part of a mighty and victorious force. Your Commander-in-Chief is the Lord of Hosts. Even then, many battles and difficulties will come your way. But as a courageous member of God's army, you will overcome.

What is a good, pursuing soldier of Christ? E. M. Bounds, an anointed Christian writer of the 1800s, said:

> The Christian soldier must be a soldier by birth, by fortune, by trade. The most essential quality of a divine soldier is that he is not entangled "with the affairs of this life" (2 Timothy 2:4). The elements of self denial, courage, and endurance are the vital characteristics of this military training.[2]

God places His strength inside you, as tempered steel, not only so you can endure during times of hardship, but also for you to stand strong, pursue, fight, and win in the mighty name of Jesus. The key is that you must stand and fight. You cannot win if you sit and do nothing. You must be determined to stand in faith upon God's Word and to act according to God's will to win the battle.

The second you move in faith, your enemies will begin to fear. Deuteronomy says, *"This day will I begin to put the dread of thee and the fear of thee upon the nations that are under the whole heaven"* (2:25). God will cause your enemies to become timid, get cold feet, and have second thoughts about fighting you when they see your faith in God. The devil is afraid of believers full of fire and the Holy Ghost who are fervent in Spirit. Satan knows that they are pursuing God's purpose for their lives, and he can not resist the name of Jesus.

Three Keys to Godly Pursuit

You will face opposition; you will meet resistance. You must overcome the challenges you face. Philippians 3:13–14 gives three keys for obtaining all that God has promised you: *"Brethren, I count not myself to have apprehended: but this one thing I do, forgetting those things which are behind, and reaching forth unto those things which are before, I press toward the mark for the prize of the high calling of God in Christ Jesus."*

Let's look at these three important keys to receiving what God has promised you:

1. **Forget what is behind you and what has happened in the past.** If you are living in the past, you will not be able to press into anything.

2. **Reach forward to what is ahead or stretch out to attain your promise.** Let your faith in God flourish. Stretch beyond what you have believed before knowing the everlasting arms of the Lord surround you.

3. **Press toward the mark.** The Greek word for "press toward" means to reach with all your might. When you reach it, you start pushing against it. Allow nothing to keep you back from what belongs to you in Christ.

Smith Wigglesworth, a hero of the faith, said:

> I have thought a great deal about momentum. I find there is such a thing as trusting in the past. When a train has gotten to a certain place, some people get out, but some go on to the end of the journey. Let us go far enough. There is only one thing to do: stay fully aware and always be pressing in. It will not do to trust in the past. Let us go forward. [3]

When you step out in faith, you are not alone. God's angels will be there with you, for they accompany warriors in Christ who are on the move. Exodus 23:20 says, *"Behold, I send an Angel before thee, to keep thee in the way, and to bring thee into the place which I have prepared."* The secret to pursuit is moving forward in faith, no matter what happens.

Pursuit Based on Faith and Hope

The devil's success is dependent upon Christians' lack of knowledge. The Bible declares, *"My people are destroyed for lack of knowledge"* (Hosea 4:6). You must know what the Bible says so that you can have faith during times of trouble.

Those who have "head faith" are not grounded and panic in times of trouble. Some people call it head faith, or hope, but it is really not even hope. Head faith is produced by man's mind and the flesh. There is no trust of God within it.

Hope and faith are two entirely different things. Faith is the substance of things hoped for. Why? Because hope takes care of tomorrow, and faith takes care of today. Hope is always in the future and is mental. Hope is in the mind, not in the heart. Hope is good, but it must not be confused with faith. Some people say, "Oh, I hope so." That is nice, but "hoping so" is not faith. Hope deals with tomorrow, or the future, and faith deals with today, or the present.

As 1 Thessalonians 5:8 says, *"But let us, who are of the day, be sober, putting on the breastplate of faith and love; and for an helmet, the hope of salvation."* Hope keeps faith alive, and faith will keep you today.

Faith comes from the heart and is produced by the Holy Ghost when we hear the Word of God. Romans 10:10 says, *"For with the heart man believeth unto righteousness; and with the mouth confession is made unto salvation."* With the heart, man believes. Heart faith becomes a part of you.

Smith Wigglesworth said:

> Faith is the Word of God. It is the personal inward flow of divine favor, which moves in every fiber of our being until our whole nature is so quickened that we live by faith, we move by faith, and we are going to be caught up to glory by faith, for faith is the victory! Faith is the glorious knowledge of a personal presence within you, changing you from strength to strength, from glory to glory, until you get to the place where you walk with God, and God thinks and speaks through you by the power of the Holy Spirit.[4]

As you pursue in faith, understand that nothing becomes dynamic in life until it becomes specific. For example, think about electricity or vast amounts of water that, once channeled, produce great power. Our lives are the same way; we must be focused to have great results.

For great results to come out of your life, you must hear the Word of God, read the Word, protect the Word, keep the Word, and make sure your life is filled with the Word. Proverbs 4:20–22 says, *"My son, attend to my words; incline thine ear unto my sayings. Let them not depart from thine eyes; keep them in the midst of thine heart. For they are life unto those that find them, and health to all their flesh."*

As you build your life upon God's Word, asking will be a natural outcome. Prayer and meditation upon God's Word activates your faith. James 4:2 says, *"Ye have not, because ye ask not."* Faith is not faith until it expects an answer. The psalmist said, *"My voice shalt thou hear in the morning, O LORD; in the morning will I direct my prayer unto thee, and will look up"* (Psalm 5:3). Looking up implies that you are expecting an answer to your prayers.

As you pray, ask God in full assurance that He will hear and answer you. James 1:6 says, *"But let him ask in faith, nothing wavering. For he that wavereth is like a wave of the sea driven with the wind and tossed."* Build your prayers upon the Rock, the Lord Jesus, by placing your faith in God's unfailing Word.

The reason some do not receive is that they do not realize that they must press in for themselves. Most people will say, "Please pray for me," not understanding that their breakthrough will happen if they will go after the promises of God for themselves.

You must go yourself and stand in faith to obtain your promise in Jesus's name. Each one of us must approach the throne for ourself and ask in faith.

The prayer of faith brings your answer and your recovery. You must take the promise of God into prayer and say, "Lord, Your Word says," and claim that promise. Keep knocking on heaven's door until it opens, and do not give up.

So many times we give up when the answer is so close. You may wonder, "Well why does God delay?" God waits to see how serious you are about getting what He promised you. The key is to believe that the process is happening while you are praying; believe that you are receiving. Mark 11:24 says, *"What things soever ye desire, when ye pray, believe that ye receive them, and ye shall have them."* Faith moves, acts, and lives as you pray.

Sometimes people mistake faith for being something that is mental. Faith is not earthly; it is a heavenly power that is birthed by the Spirit through reading the Word of God. Romans 10:17 says, *"So then faith cometh by hearing, and hearing by the word of God."* As you read the Word, the Spirit of God will put life into that *logos* (written) word, and it will become a *rhema* (revealed) word in your soul. At that point, the Word becomes alive, and it has living faith.

Isaiah 60:1 exhorts, *"Arise, shine; for thy light is come, and the glory of the LORD is risen upon thee."* God declares He will cause you to ride upon the high places of the earth. You are on top, not on the bottom. God declared through Moses that you would lend and not borrow. You are the head, not the tail. You are above, not beneath. You are a person of victory!

As you delight yourself in the Lord, He will cause you to ride upon the high places of the earth. Isaiah 49:17 contains a promise to do with your children and your family: *"Thy children shall make haste; thy destroyers and they that made thee waste shall go forth of thee."* Your children are going to come to God, and the enemy that stole from you and made you empty is going to leave your life.

The Word of God is filled with promise after promise of your recovery. God wants to see you whole in every area of your life. He intends for you to live abundantly today!

RECOVERY WITHOUT MEASURE

You can have an even greater anointing upon your life than Elisha had with his double-portion anointing. In 1 John 2:27 we read: *"But the anointing which ye have received of him abideth in you, and ye need not that any man teach you: but as the same anointing teacheth you of all things, and is truth, and is no lie, and even as it hath taught you, ye shall abide in him."*

You have received the anointing of Jesus. The double-portion anointing is good, but there is more. The anointing that Jesus had is the anointing without measure. We must never settle for less than God's greatest promise for our lives. Jesus said, *"With men this is impossible; but with God all things are possible"* (Matthew 19:26).

Ezekiel 12:28 declares, *"There shall none of my words be prolonged any more, but the word which I have spoken shall be done, saith the Lord GOD."* God says, "What I promise, I will do." The Lord is faithful to perform His Word, and it is your job as His child to believe it and receive it.

As Christians, we should live an ongoing life of glory. God desires for your walk with Him to be an ever-expanding walk that continually grows from dimension to dimension.

Romans 1:17 teaches: *"For therein is the righteousness of God revealed from faith to faith: as it is written, The just shall live by faith."* God Almighty is an ongoing God. He is always moving, and heaven itself is a place of progression.

Smith Wigglesworth wrote: "There is only one way to all the treasures of God, and that is the way of faith. All things are possible, even the fulfilling of all promises is possible, to him who believes." [5]

MORE THAN A CONQUEROR

God the Father is the source of faith. Jesus is the Word of faith. The Holy Ghost is the substance of faith. Faith comes to you when the Spirit of God is welcomed into your life. The Holy Spirit brings faith to you;

it is His gift. When the Holy Ghost comes into your life, faith comes with Him and rests in your heart, because He is the Spirit of faith.

In 2 Corinthians 5:7 we're taught: *"For we walk by faith, not by sight."* Another mighty promise is found in 1 John 5:4, which says, *"For whatsoever is born of God overcometh the world: and this is the victory that overcometh the world, even our faith."*

God told David he would *"without fail recover all."* God has destined you to be a victorious overcomer in this world. All you must do is allow faith in God's precious Word to fill every part of your heart. God really wants you to recover all, and total recovery can be yours today as you pursue God's will, no matter what happens to you.

I love the many examples of pursuit and recovery throughout the Bible. One is the story of Benaiah:

> *Benaiah the son of Jehoiada, the son of a valiant man of Kabzeel, who had done many acts; he slew two lionlike men of Moab: also he went down and slew a lion in a pit in a snowy day. And he slew an Egyptian, a man of great stature, five cubits high; and in the Egyptian's hand was a spear like a weaver's beam; and he went down to him with a staff, and plucked the spear out of the Egyptian's hand, and slew him with his own spear.* (1 Chronicles 11:22–23)

Benaiah slew two lionlike men with his own hands. The Egyptian had a sophisticated weapon, and all Benaiah had was a piece of wood, but he had God on his side.

Remember, the same thing happened with David and Goliath. The giant had the latest, overpowering weaponry. He had a monstrous size advantage. David had only five little stones, a sling, and faith, yet he slew the great giant.

The fearful say, "This job, circumstance, or problem is too big. I cannot do it." All of Israel thought Goliath was too big for David to win, but David apparently thought, "Goliath is so big that I can't miss!"

Isaiah 41:10 says, *"Fear thou not; for I am with thee: be not dismayed; for I am thy God: I will strengthen thee; yea, I will help thee; yea, I will uphold thee with the right hand of my righteousness."* God promises to keep you. He will never allow you to be ashamed or confounded. God is your Redeemer, and He will help you. You must simply decide that you are going to arise and possess the land that He has given you.

A FINAL NOTE

It is time to pursue all that God has set in store for us. Psalm 108:13 states: *"Through God we shall do valiantly: for he it is that shall tread down our enemies."* Faith in action can accomplish great things for the kingdom of God.

Daniel 11:32 says that you will be strong and *"do exploits."* Whatever enemy and obstacle has held you back, stolen from you, and caused you sorrow must flee away in the name of Jesus.

You must put your faith into action: *"For whatsoever is born of God overcometh the world: and this is the victory that overcometh the world, even our faith. Who is he that overcometh the world, but he that believeth that Jesus is the Son of God?"* (1 John 5:4–5).

You can gain victory! You can say, "With God's help, I can overcome!" God promises to help you overcome whatever you face as you seek His direction: *"Fear thou not; for I am with thee: be not dismayed; for I am thy God: I will strengthen thee; yea, I will help thee; yea, I will uphold thee with the right hand of my righteousness"* (Isaiah 41:10).

God is your Redeemer, and He will help you. The Lord is with you as He was with David and his 3-D army. God has ordained that you recover all, be victorious, and be more than a conqueror. And God has already given you everything you need to do that.

David pursued his enemies by acting upon what God said to him. When the Lord said "pursue" David pursued. David put his faith into action and he followed through with what God had spoken for Him to do. He did not sit idly or slothfully, hoping and wishing for something to happen. He pursued his enemy. As a result, God gave him the victory.

Pursue!

5

TOTAL RECOVERY
THROUGH POWER

And David recovered all that the Amaleites had carried away.

—1 SAMUEL 30:16

David's band, the motley 3-D crew in distress, debt, and discontent, were undoubtedly outcasts who had nowhere else to go. Those who had served with him before were in danger. As they joined together in the cave, they probably were filled with the futility of standing against Saul's army or the Amalekites.

Who would want to train such an army? Who could hope for anything but more problems by being associated with these men?

Yet, let's fast-forward. Because of God's total-recovery program of praise, prayer, and pursuit, the army became extremely powerful. The Bible spotlights three of these former 3-D men:

These be the names of the mighty men whom David had: The
Tachmonite that sat in the seat, chief among the captains; the
same was Adino the Eznite: he lift up his spear against eight
hundred, whom he slew at one time. And after him was Eleazar
the son of Dodo the Ahohite, one of the three mighty men with
David, when they defied the Philistines that were there gathered

together to battle, and the men of Israel were gone away: He arose, and smote the Philistines until his hand was weary, and his hand clave unto the sword: and the LORD *wrought a great victory that day; and the people returned after him only to spoil. And after him was Shammah the son of Agee the Hararite. And the Philistines were gathered together into a troop, where was a piece of ground full of lentiles: and the people fled from the Philistines. But he stood in the midst of the ground, and defended it, and slew the Philistines: and the* LORD *wrought a great victory.* (2 Samuel 23:8–12)

Let's focus on these three men featured in this passage of Scripture:

- **Adino the Eznite**—the name Adino means "his spear" in Hebrew. Adino killed 800 men with his spear in one single battle. That is no small feat in any day, especially in a time of hand-to-hand, metal-against-flesh conflict. Can you imagine?
- **Eleazar**—Eleazar, "God's helper," apparently stood against an entire force of Philistines by himself. The other men had gone away, possibly to another part of the battle. Eleazar, impossibly outmanned, used his sword in battle until he couldn't peel his hand away from the bloody weapon. Amazingly, after the battle was over, the rest of Eleazar's forces returned in time to take part in the spoils of victory.
- **Shammah**—His name means "astonishing." He stood in the middle of a bean patch and heard his own forces running away in fear, yet Shammah refused to cower. It is no wonder the 3-D soldiers fled, for historians say the Philistines were the most modern and best naturally equipped army of that day. Shammah's victory that day is legendary enough to be included in God's Holy Word. We

are told expressly that the Lord was with Shammah as he fought an entire Philistine troop.

How did these three men—formerly imprisoned in distress, debt, and discontent—find a way to become such mighty warriors in David's army? More importantly, how did these three leaders who refused to flee become such integral parts of an army that would eventually become the most feared and successful throughout the region?

Somehow, despite all the odds, these men were transformed through David's teaching and leadership. That teaching focused on honoring and obeying God. In return, the Creator gave David and his followers the authority to do mighty exploits.

AUTHORITY

Before you can attack the enemy's camp, you must know your authority as a believer. I've heard someone say, "Any soldier running into the enemy's camp naked is a fool." We cannot afford to be foolish when it comes to recovery.

You must not run into the enemy's camp unarmed and unprepared. Remember, the devil's success is dependent on ignorance of believers. Therefore, you must be very wise, full of the Word of God, and full of His power.

You pursue and penetrate the enemy's camp by taking back what it took from you. David was full of God's Word. He knew his authority as God's child, and he acted upon that knowledge against the warring tribe who had stolen everything from him:

> *And when he had brought him down, behold, they were spread abroad upon all the earth, eating and drinking, and dancing,*

because of all the great spoil that they had taken out of the land
of the Philistines, and out of the land of Judah. And David
smote them from the twilight even unto the evening of the next
day: and there escaped not a man of them, save four hundred
young men, which rode upon camels, and fled. And David
recovered all that the Amalekites had carried away: and David
rescued his two wives. And there was nothing lacking to them,
neither small nor great, neither sons nor daughters, neither spoil,
nor any thing that they had taken to them: David recovered all.
And David took all the flocks and the herds, which they drave
before those other cattle, and said, this is David's spoil.
(1 Samuel 30:16–20)

There was nothing lacking for David after he attacked the Amalekites and took back what belonged to him. God restored everything that was lost to David, and God can do the same for you. The Word says, *"David recovered all."*

As you study the account of this battle against the Amalekites, you can read how an Egyptian led David straight to the enemy's camp. The Word of God says that David came upon his enemies while they were eating, drinking, and dancing. They were unprepared, not knowing that David and his army were about to show up.

Often, sadly, the enemy comes upon God's children when we are unaware. It should be the other way around. God wants you to be prepared to pursue and penetrate the enemy's camp to recover all that has been stolen from you.

Luke 11:21–22 says, *"When a strong man armed keepeth his palace, his goods are in peace: But when a stronger than he shall come upon him, and overcome him, he taketh from him all his armour wherein he trusted, and divideth his spoils."* The words "come upon" in this passage mean to overtake your enemy when he is not looking. If the enemy knows you are coming, he will prepare. When he does not know to expect you he is caught off guard and unprepared.

ALL POWER

God has given you all power over the enemy. Every part of satan's kingdom is under your feet: *"No weapon that is formed against thee shall prosper; and every tongue that shall rise against thee in judgment thou shalt condemn. This is the heritage of the servants of the LORD, and their righteousness is of me, saith the LORD"* (Isaiah 54:17).

God has given incredible clout to those who understand the principles of total recovery: *"Behold, I give unto you power to tread on serpents and scorpions, and over all the power of the enemy: and nothing shall by any means hurt you"* (Luke 10:19). Notice that we are given all power, not partial power. The Word says so! The enemy will try to attack you, but you have a shield of faith all around you. Satan's missiles can't penetrate God's shield.

The great writer E. M. Bounds said: "The devil lets his fiery, poisoned darts fly, but faith catches them as they are directed at head or heart, and quenches them."[1] The key is that you must be armed and protected by following the promises of God's Word. These promises lead to supernatural power.

There are several different Greek words which are translated as "power." One of them is *dunamis*, which means "power that reproduces itself." Another is the word we use for "authority," which is "power to command, influence, and administrate." Another word for "power" in Greek is *exusia*, meaning "delegated authority." The Lord Jesus has given you the right to stand in His stead and proclaim His victory in your situation and liberty to those who are captive.

Not only do you have His promised authority, the Word of God also clearly declares that the devil has already been defeated. The Son of God, Jesus Christ, destroyed the works of the devil and triumph is yours today.

Jesus won the victory, and you have been given the privilege to enforce that victory, to administer that victory, to execute it, and to exercise it. The devil was given the spoil by Adam through sin, but today total recovery is yours by promise through Christ Jesus.

God's power is released through you because of His Word in you. It is because of God's Word that the enemy is defeated: *"Then the LORD put forth his hand, and touched my mouth. And the LORD said unto me, Behold, I have put my words in thy mouth. See, I have this day set thee over the nations and over the kingdoms, to root out, and to pull down, and to destroy, and to throw down, to build, and to plant"* (Jeremiah 1:9–10).

God's Word *in* you produces God's purpose *through* you. In fact, He has promised that the enemy will not prevail against you: *"And they shall fight against thee; but they shall not prevail against thee; for I am with thee, saith the LORD, to deliver thee"* (Jeremiah 1:19).

The courts of heaven are higher and greater than the courts of hell, and the law of God is greater than the law of satan. When you pray, God says to the devil, "Let the one who is bound go!" and the devil must obey. Prayer destroys the legality of satan; the Bible says that the prey of the terrible shall be delivered. God has given you mighty authority as a believer.

The Name Above Every Name

God's power and authority is tied into His precious name. God wants His people to know Him and to walk in under His protection and influence. The very power that raised Jesus from the dead and put Him above all powers and principalities belongs to you. Yet in order to be victorious, you must know who you are in Christ.

When the name of Jesus Christ is mentioned, every enemy must bow. Some people think that this Scripture is for the future, but when Jesus rose from the dead He said, *"All power is given unto me in heaven and in earth"* (Matthew 28:18).

When you speak His name, every knee shall bow. Every authority will submit to the power in His name. In the book of Luke, the authority in Jesus's name amazed His followers: *"And the seventy returned again with joy, saying, Lord, even the devils are subject unto us through thy name"* (Luke 10:17). The disciples returned saying, *"In thy name devils come out and we have power."*

What was the Savior's response? It is very clear-cut: *"Notwithstanding in this rejoice not, that the spirits are subject unto you; but rather rejoice, because your names are written in heaven"* (Luke 10:20).

Jesus has been given a name above every name: *"Wherefore God also hath highly exalted him, and given him a name which is above every name: That at the name of Jesus every knee should bow, of things in heaven, and things in earth, and things under the earth"* (Philippians 2:9–10).

As you say, "In the name of Jesus," you are expressing your God-given authority over the enemy. God's mighty power will flow through you, and you will experience breakthrough and total recovery.

BUILDING AND BATTLING

Two things always go hand in hand with authority: building and battling. Matthew 16:18 says, *"Upon this rock I will build my church; and the gates of hell shall not prevail against it."* The church must be built up before it can go into battle.

The question then becomes, Well, how do we build ourselves up so nothing will prevail against us? The Word of God and prayer build us up. Paul clearly states that the word of God's grace *"is able to build you up, and to give you an inheritance among all them which are sanctified"* (Acts 20:32). The Bible also states that the Word of God effectually works *"in you that believe"* (1 Thessalonians 2:13). As you read God's Word and are filled with faith, you become a strong believer; and as you call upon the Lord in prayer, you will be filled with fire so that no enemy can defeat you.

You will be built up as you fill your life with God's Word, the anointing of the Spirit, and prayer. Jude 20–21 says, *"But ye, beloved, building up yourselves on your most holy faith, praying in the Holy Ghost, Keep yourselves in the love of God, looking for the mercy of our Lord Jesus Christ unto eternal life."*

Ephesians 6:10 commissions: *"Be strong in the Lord, and in the power of his might."* Notice that this passage says, *"In the Lord."* Remember that you must remain near Him, close to Him, and find your sufficiency in Him. We can't do it without Him. If you are empty of God's Word, you will also be empty of His power. If you are prayerless, you will also be powerless.

How can you fight and win if you do not pray? Our strength must never be in ourselves but always in the Lord our God. When that happens, we can recover all.

POSSESSING THE GATES OF THE ENEMY

As we discuss authority and recovery, let's get very specific. God gave Abraham a mighty promise that his seed would flourish: *"That in blessing I will bless thee, and in multiplying I will multiply thy seed as the stars of the heaven, and as the sand which is upon the sea shore; and thy seed shall possess the gate of his enemies"* (Genesis 22:17). The Hebrew word for "possess" means "to control, to have power over, or to have authority over."

What did it mean for Abraham to have authority over the gates of the enemy?

Gates are symbolic of spiritual power and authority. Gates speak of rule. Gates also speak of the place of counsel. Proverbs talks about gates in a number of passages, referring to that place where people would sit to receive counsel or advice from the elders in the gates. Those who sat in the gates were people who knew counsel, and who understood laws and regulations.

Galatians 3:29 declares: *"If ye be Christ's, then are ye Abraham's seed, and heirs according to the promise."* The promise that God gave to Abraham belongs to you. You will possess the gates of the enemy as you recover all.

As a believer, you not only have power over the authorities and rulers of hell, but you also have power over the counsel of the enemy. You can destroy his plans. Jesus said, *"Upon this rock I will build my church; and the gates of hell shall not prevail against it"* (Matthew 16:18). Satan's plans will not overwhelm you.

God has promised that His plan will be established in your life.

The devil may plan things against you, but they will not prosper. Isaiah 54:17 promises, *"No weapon that is formed against thee shall prosper."* He is continually planning to attack you and planning to destroy you, but his plans will come to naught if you are full of the Word of God and remain in prayer.

When you are ready to attack the gate of your enemy, God will give you strength for battle. Isaiah 28:5-6 says, *"In that day shall the Lord of hosts be for a crown of glory, and for a diadem of beauty, unto the residue of his people, And for a spirit of judgment to him that sitteth in judgment, and for strength to them that turn the battle to the gate."*

This passage shows that the Lord wants His people to turn their weapons away from one another and instead battle the enemy at the gate.

Your battle is not against flesh and blood. Victory and success in the natural are dependent upon victory and success in the spirit realm.

David understood authority in the spirit. Although Saul repeatedly chased him, David submitted himself to God's authority. He respected the anointing that God had placed on Saul and would not lift his hand against him. He knew his battle was not against flesh and blood.

Wrote the powerful twentieth-century Chinese teacher Watchman Nee: "If men are to serve God, subjection to authority is absolute necessity. Obedience transcends our work. Should David rule his kingdom but fail to be subject to God's authority, he would be as useless as Saul."[2]

Never think the devil has ultimate power on earth. The Lord Jesus said, *"All power is given unto me in heaven and in earth"* (Matthew 28:18). The reason the devil is able to cause havoc is that the church does not stand up and resist him. If you look at history, you will see that the devil has convinced the church that we are powerless so he can step in and take over. God gave all power to Jesus, and Jesus gave His power to the church, saying we should go and teach the nations. As God's people submit to Jesus's authority, we are given authority.

You should never be afraid of the enemy, because you belong to the Lord. He is able to keep you, and He alone is the Rock who girds you with strength and makes your feet strong and sure, as with hinds feet (see Psalm 18:31–33). Only the Lord can preserve you and set you safely in a high place.

You need not fear if you trust the Savior. God's kingdom is an everlasting kingdom. Watchman Nee also said this: "The kingdom of David continues until now; even the Lord Jesus is a descendant of David."[3] Isaiah 41:10 uplifts: *"Fear thou not; for I am with thee: be not dismayed; for I am thy God: I will strengthen thee; yea, I will help thee; yea, I will uphold thee with the right hand of my righteousness."*

Celebrate the Victory

Christ causes us to triumph, and it is up to the body of Christ to enforce the victory that He won on Calvary's cross. You see, a triumph is not a victory, but it is the celebration of the victory! Christ has won your battles, and so you must rejoice in that the victory is won. Christ defeated the enemy of your souls, but it is up to you to enforce it.

The devil is called the strongman, but Jesus Christ is much stronger. Jesus came and disarmed him; the Lord took satan's armor away and divided his spoils. The works of the devil are destroyed in your life. Jesus, by His work on Calvary, set you free.

In Colossians 2:15 the Word says that the enemy has been defused by Christ: *"And having spoiled principalities and powers, he made a shew of them openly, triumphing over them in it."* When David pursued and penetrated the enemy's camp, he took the spoils and divided them. All knew that the enemy had been defeated, and God answered David's prayers by bringing total recovery.

The enemy's spoils have been divided, and the goods are yours. Throughout the Bible, you will never find satan carrying a sword. There is not one Scripture that says the devil is carrying anything. All that he has against you are words, powerless against the Word. You have been given a mighty weapon to fight him with—the sword of the Spirit. Ephesians 6:17 declares, *"And take…the sword of the Spirit, which is the word of God."*

All that has been stolen from you has been recovered. It is waiting for you to claim. All that the devil took from you has been restored to you again through the work of redemption at the Cross. Power is promised to you. The power of God that raised Jesus from the dead is yours as a believer. It is already available to you, and it is ready for a specific reason.

You Are the Light of the World

Our great commission as believers in Jesus Christ is to take the mighty message of the Gospel into all the earth. We are to share it with all nations, *"baptizing them in the name of the Father, and of the Son, and of the Holy Ghost"* (Matthew 28:19) and teaching them to observe the Lord's commandments (see verse 20).

It is the church's job to build people up in the knowledge of the Lord. The Lord promises to go with you as you spread His Word. He stands right there with you, backing you up as you enforce His victory.

Matthew 28:20 says, *"I am with you alway, even unto the end of the world."* The Lord Jesus is counting on you and me to tell others about His love. The Lord knows that when His church truly fulfills the Great Commission, great recovery and revival will come.

Revelation 12:11 declares: *"And they overcame him by the blood of the Lamb, and by the word of their testimony; and they loved not their lives unto the death."* Your testimony and the knowledge of what the Lord Jesus has done for you holds mighty power. As you share the truth that God has put in your heart, it will bring souls out of darkness and into light, out of bondage and into the liberty of Christ.

What brings the Gospel into the world? Believers do—you and I do. You are a carrier of the living Word of God, and you have the answer the world needs. How will the people of the world know they can recover all and be set free from bondage unless you tell them that Christ Jesus has given them power to penetrate the enemy's camp?

A Final Note

The Bible reveals how all power on heaven and earth belongs to the Lord Jesus (see Matthew 28:18). The reason the devil causes havoc is that the church does not stand up and resist him. Looking at history, we see that the devil has convinced the church that we are powerless so that he can step in and take over. But God gave all power to Jesus, and Jesus gave His power to the church, telling us to go and teach the nations. As God's people submit to Jesus's authority, we are given authority. So we don't need to fear if we trust in Him. God's kingdom is an everlasting kingdom.

When David attacked the enemy's camp, he took the spoils away and divided them. There was no mixed message. Everyone in the area knew that the Amalekites had been defeated. God answered David's prayers and brought him total recovery.

Likewise, in the spiritual realm, the enemy's spoils have been divided and the goods are yours. It is finished! You will never find in the Bible satan carrying a sword. Not one scripture in the Bible says the devil is carrying anything except words. We have been given a mighty weapon to counteract the enemy's words—His Word: *"The sword of the Spirit, which is the word of God"* (Ephesians 6:17).

All that has been stolen from you is recovered. All that the devil took from you, through the cross of Jesus, has been restored to you again. Power for total recovery is promised to you! Now you must take it.

You have the authority in the Name that is above all names. Now it is up to you to use it!

6

TOTAL RECOVERY
OF YOUR FAMILY

❖❖❖

And David recovered all that the Amalekites had carried away . . .
And there was nothing lacking to them, neither small nor great, neither
sons nor daughters, neither spoil, nor any thing that they had taken to
them: David recovered all.

—1 Samuel 30:18–19

G od has promised that the enemy will not prevail against you
or your family. Jeremiah 1:19 says, *"And they shall fight*
against thee; but they shall not prevail against thee; for I am
with thee, saith the LORD, to deliver thee."

Look at Isaiah 49:24–25: *"Shall the prey be taken from the mighty, or*
the lawful captive delivered? But thus saith the LORD, Even the captives of
the mighty shall be taken away, and the prey of the terrible shall be deliv-
ered: for I will contend with him that contendeth with thee, and I will
save thy children." God will fight with the enemy of you and your family. He will save your children!

The courts of heaven are higher and greater than the courts of hell,
and the law of God is greater than the law of satan. When you pray, God
says to the devil, "Let the one who is bound go!" and the devil must obey.
Prayer destroys satan's power. God has given you mighty authority as a

believer. No name is greater than the name of Jesus. All of hell cannot stand against Him, especially when the enemy attacks a believer's family.

A Foundation for Total Recovery

This foundational principle didn't start with the Passover. Even back in Genesis 7:1, the Bible declares, *"And the LORD said unto Noah, Come thou and all thy house into the ark; for thee have I seen righteous before me in this generation."*

I remember asking a group of young people, "Why do you think God asked Noah to build the ark?"

"To save all the animals," was their immediate response.

No. He prepared it for his family. Noah, *"being warned of God of things not seen as yet, moved with fear, prepared an ark to the saving of his house"* (Hebrews 11:7). What faith Noah must have had! People living in his day had not seen water fall from the sky, and this man declared, "It is going to rain, and the whole world will be flooded!"

Quickly, he began building an ark to save his family from something he could hardly describe.

"Oh, you foolish man," the people must have laughed.

Before this time, rain had never fallen upon the earth. The earth had been gently watered by the dew. Imagine what the wicked people of that generation must have thought when Noah began to preach about the flood and the peril that was coming. At first they dismissed Noah's warnings, but as he continued, they probably asked, "What is he talking about?"

Noah told everyone who would listen that it was going to rain and flood the earth. He had total faith in something he did not fully understand and began building an ark to save his family from something he could not even describe.

In a world filled with iniquity, there was only one person who found grace in the eyes of the Lord: *"But Noah found grace in the eyes of the LORD"* (Genesis 6:8). As a result, we know that his family escaped the flood, for the Lord said to Noah, *"Come thou and all thy house into the ark; for thee have I seen righteous before me in this generation"* (Genesis 7:1).

God saw only Noah as pure and virtuous, yet his family was rescued. I believe when you are righteous before the Lord, your entire family will be touched by God's amazing grace. Centuries later, Peter wrote that God *"spared not the old world, but saved Noah the eighth person, a preacher of righteousness, bringing in the flood upon the world of the ungodly"* (2 Peter 2:5).

Eight people were spared? Noah's three sons (Shem, Ham, and Japeth) and their wives, Noah's wife, and Noah—the eighth person. God placed him last, showing clearly that all of his children, even though unrighteous, were included in His righteousness.

Is the Lord concerned about your family, regardless of their spiritual condition right now? You can count on it! It is a foundation throughout the Bible.

ABRAHAM'S INFLUENCE

Abraham was a righteous man who knew how to talk to God. Abraham and his nephew Lot lived on the same land for some time. When it became too crowded for them to dwell together, Lot was given the choice of where to live. He chose Sodom, an extremely wicked, worldly place.

Later, God forewarned Abraham that He was going to destroy Sodom. Lot went about his daily routine in wicked Sodom totally unaware of God's visit to Abraham, warning him of the coming danger. Abraham began to intercede for the wicked city of Sodom because of his nephew. In Genesis 18:23–25 he reasoned with God saying, *"Would You also destroy the righteous with the wicked? Suppose there were fifty righteous within the city, would You also destroy the place and not spare it for the fifty righteous that were in it?... Shall not the Judge of all the earth do right?"* (NKJV).

Paraphrasing, the Lord said, "If I find fifty righteous within the city of Sodom, I will spare the place for their sakes."

"What if there aren't fifty righteous, but only forty-five?" Abraham asked. "Will you destroy them with the wicked?"

Again the Lord said, "If I find forty-five righteous, I will not destroy Sodom."

"What about forty?" Abraham continued. "Would you destroy Sodom if there are forty righteous there?"

Once again the Lord responded that He would not destroy the righteous with the wicked if there were only forty righteous found.

Abraham continued this conversation in prayer with the Lord, asking if God would destroy Sodom if only thirty righteous were found, then if only twenty righteous were found, and finally if only ten righteous could be found. So Sodom was destroyed.

God spared Lot's family from the destruction because of Abraham's position with God. Genesis 19:29 declares, *"And it came to pass, when God destroyed the cities of the plain, that God remembered Abraham, and sent Lot out of the midst of the overthrow, when he overthrew the cities in which Lot had dwelt."*

Because of Abraham's walk with God—not Lot's—Lot was spared from Sodom's destruction, because Abraham was an intercessor on his behalf. God will also rescue your loved ones from the clutches of the enemy because of your faith.

Do you have loved ones who have chosen the worldly "Sodoms" in which to dwell? We are all Abraham's children according to Galatians

3:29 which says: *"And if ye be Christ's then are ye Abraham's seed, and heirs according to the promise."* As Abraham's seed, we have inherited the privilege of walking as intercessors. As a believer, you must begin to intercede for your loved ones. And when you do, God will begin to rescue the "Lots" in your family!

If you desire to see people come to Christ, become an intercessor . . . for the world, for your city, and for your loved ones. God will rescue them for your sake.

Do you realize that you are the seed of Abraham? If you have been born again, you now possess this special position.

If you are a believer, every "Lot" in your family—a son, daughter, nephew, niece, aunt, uncle or cousin—is important to God. Become an intercessor and He will look upon them with grace. Your relationship with the Lord affects your loved ones.

MORE OLD TESTAMENT HOUSEHOLD RECOVERIES

God commanded Moses to speak to the people of Israel, saying, *"On the tenth day of this month every man shall take for himself a lamb, according to the house of his father, a lamb for a household"* (Exodus 12:3, NKJV). During the Passover feast, it is the tradition that every Jewish family take one lamb for a family—and if one man partakes, all can partake. The lamb is available for the entire house.

Exodus 12:3–4 points to an amazing principle foretold during the Passover, then fulfilled through the Lamb of God:

> *Speak ye unto all the congregation of Israel, saying, In the tenth day of this month they shall take to them every man a lamb, according to the house of their fathers, a lamb for an house: And if the household be too little for the lamb, let him and his*

neighbour next unto his house take it according to the number
of the souls; every man according to his eating shall make your
count for the lamb.

God's intention from the very first Passover was for a lamb to be sacrificed for each house. It wasn't a lamb for each person. The shed blood was to cover every person in the household. It wasn't just the father, but fathers. It wasn't just the mother, but mothers. The protection included uncles, aunts, cousins. And if you will look at verse 4, the neighbors could even be protected by the shed blood of the lamb.

Certainly, every person in the household had the free choice of whether to stay in the house which was protected by the blood, just as each individual in a house has free will whether to accept Jesus Christ as Savior. However, it is God's desire to protect the entire household.

Today, if one person receives Jesus—the Lamb of God—the Savior is available for all in that dwelling.

In Joshua 24:15, we read: *"And if it seem evil unto you to serve the* LORD, *choose you this day whom ye will serve; whether the gods which your fathers served that were on the other side of the flood, or the gods of the Amorites, in whose land ye dwell: but as for me and my house, we will serve the* LORD.*"* Joshua made the decision to serve God, and his decision affected his household.

Are you beginning to grasp how your family has special privileges because you have been saved?

NEW TESTAMENT HOUSEHOLD SALVATIONS AND RECOVERIES

Now look in the New Testament. Acts 16:14–15 shares the story of the Lydia, a new believer in Jesus, and what happened to her household:

A seller of purple, of the city of Thyatira, which worshipped God, heard us: whose heart the Lord opened, that she attended unto the things which were spoken of Paul. And when she was baptized, and her household, she besought us, saying, If ye have judged me to be faithful to the Lord, come into my house, and abide there. And she constrained us.

Recorded later in that same chapter, the Philippian jailer became not only a new believer but also witnessed the miracle of his family becoming believers as well:

Sirs, what must I do to be saved? And they said, Believe on the Lord Jesus Christ, and thou shalt be saved, and thy house. And they spake unto him the word of the Lord, and to all that were in his house. And he took them the same hour of the night, and washed their stripes; and was baptized, he and all his, straight-way. And when he had brought them into his house, he set meat before them, and rejoiced, believing in God with all his house. (Acts 16:30–34)

Acts 18:8 shares a similar account: *"And Crispus, the chief ruler of the synagogue, believed on the Lord with all his house; and many of the Corinthians hearing believed, and were baptized."* He believed with all his house!

Look for a moment at the story of Paul and Silas, who were beaten and thrown into prison for preaching the Gospel. The jailer was instructed to keep them secure, so he placed them in an inner prison and bound their feet with chains. How did Paul and Silas respond? At midnight they *"sang praises unto God: and the prisoners heard them"* (Acts 16:25). Suddenly there was a great earthquake. The foundations of the prison were shaken, and immediately all the doors were opened and everyone's chains were loosed: *"And the keeper of the prison, awaking from sleep and seeing the prison doors open, he drew out his sword and would have killed himself, supposing that the prisoners had been fled"* (Acts 16:27).

Why was the jailer about to take such drastic action? Under Roman law if you guarded a prisoner who escaped, you were required to give your life for that fugitive. It would be easier to take his own life rather than to face the courts and be killed—and if he did not, one of his family members would be substituted.

The Scriptures record that Paul called with a loud voice, saying, *"Do thyself no harm: for we are all here"* (verse 28). In the darkness, the jailer called for a light, ran in, and fell down trembling before Paul and Silas. He brought them out, saying, *"Sirs, what must I do to be saved?"* (verse 30).

Why would he ask such a question? That guard heard the two Christians singing and praising God in the night and was drawn by the Holy Spirit to seek the Savior. Then Paul and Silas gave the jailer this marvelous assurance: *"Believe on the Lord Jesus Christ, and you will be saved, you and your household"* (Acts 16:31, NKJV). Think of it! Salvation was not only for this man, but for his entire household: *"Then they spoke the word of the Lord to him and to all who were in his house"* (verse 32, NKJV).

What a mighty God we serve! And because of the principle of a lamb for a house, you have the legal right to claim every member of your family for Christ. You have the same right to claim salvation for your neighbors. The promise is yours. There is an umbrella of grace over you and your household. You can bring your entire neighborhood under the blood of the Cross and still have room for more.

When you become a believer, those closest to you cannot help but see the change that begins to happen supernaturally. They may run from the blood. They may scoff at its results. But you can win them to Christ because of the grace of God that rests on your household through the blood of the Lamb.

My Testimony

Your loved ones can be saved. I have experienced the reality of household salvation personally. Today my entire family is saved, and I am grateful to our wonderful Lord Jesus for that. But at one time, none of us was born again. I was the first one to receive salvation, and when I did, my life was totally transformed. After I accepted Jesus Christ into my life, God began moving in my family, though the process certainly didn't go well at first.

When I met Jesus at a high school student-led prayer meeting in Toronto in 1972, my family thought I had lost my mind. My father was an extremely strong-willed person from the Middle East. He was a strict disciplinarian, imposing in size, had a commanding personality, and was larger than life. He loved his family, but there was never any doubt who was in charge.

The first time I mentioned Jesus in our home after I was saved, my father warned me sternly: "Mention that name in my house once more, and you'll wish you hadn't. Forsake this experience, or we will forsake you!"

Riding with my father in the family car not long after our initial confrontation about Jesus, he tried once again to dissuade me from my stand as a Christian. He promised me different things, trying to turn me away from what I had found in Christ. One thing was always certain about my father: he never broke a promise, and he made it very clear that he was committed to making me forget "this Christian fanatical thing." When he had finished, he paused and waited for my response. I looked into his piercing eyes and replied, "There is nothing you can do to force me to forget about Jesus."

The expression on my father's face instantly revealed his anger at my response. And this wasn't the first time I had seen that expression or felt his glaring wrath. As a little boy, I had often looked up at his towering, six-foot-plus frame and felt the intimidation of his stern glare when I didn't measure up to his expectations. There in the car I had similar feelings. It was apparent that I had not pleased him; I had not given the answer he had desired. At times like that as a child I would run and hide under the bed, but that day in the car there was nowhere to hide to escape his angry, silent glare. With nothing else to say, we drove home in silence.

Needless to say, there was great tension in our family. Jesus had become the Lord of my life, yet my family just didn't understand. My grandmother (on my dad's side) was deeply concerned and began sending telegrams from Israel to my father, demanding, "You must do something about your son." She even flew to Canada in an attempt to talk me out of this "Jesus thing."

"Grandmother," I told her, "I love and respect you, but I will never forsake Jesus. And you need to know Him, too."

Things became increasingly difficult at home. My family couldn't find any logical explanation for the change they saw in me, so they just ignored me. I began to feel like an intruder in my own home, and the isolation became increasingly painful. My family begged me not to dishonor the family name by pursuing this "Jesus stuff." But the reality I had found in my relationship with Jesus Christ was more precious to me than anything. Although I loved my family, I loved my wonderful Lord Jesus more. I knew that I could not turn away from Him and His love for me.

In desperation, my father tried something else. He arranged for me to work for a friend of his. Perhaps he thought if I was busy working, I wouldn't have time to think about this "Jesus." Unsuccessful, my father finally said in despair, "Benny, what can I do for you? What do you want me to do? I'll do anything you want if you'll just forget about this Jesus of yours."

I swallowed hard and said, "Dad, you can say what you want, but I would rather die than give up what I've found in Jesus."

From that time and for nearly two years following, my father and I had almost no communication. It was as though I was invisible, and my presence was seldom acknowledged. Although my family and I lived in the same house, our relationship deteriorated to that of strangers. Only the love of Jesus Christ sustained me during those lonely times.

How did a family like this, so hardened to the Gospel message, receive salvation? As a young believer, I battled the strongholds in prayer that held my loved ones captive. As I continued to pray for each of my family members, God began to deal with them, one by one.

My sister Mary was the first one to give her heart to the Lord. Next, my brother Sammy got saved. I'll never forget the earnest prayer he prayed: "Jesus, come into my heart. Lock Yourself in, and throw away the key." Not long after that, Willie came to know Jesus as Savior. One by one they came, including my mother and father, until my entire family was saved! God even allowed me to pray with my grandmother before she passed from this life.

If God can save a family like mine, He can save yours as well. Your loved ones can be saved! Again, each family member has a free choice about receiving Jesus Christ as Savior, but one of the great revelations of God's Word is that salvation is promised not only for an individual, but for your entire household.

Salvation for Your Household

There are three important things you need to know about the salvation of your loved ones:

- It is God's will for all to be saved. The Word tells us that the Lord is *"not willing that any should perish, but that all should come to repentance"* (2 Peter 3:9).
- It is your responsibility to share your faith with the members of your household: *"He said unto them, Go ye into all the world, and preach the gospel to every creature. He that believeth and is baptized shall be saved; but he that believeth not shall be damned"* (Mark 16:15–16).
- God gives every person, even those in your household, free choice about accepting Jesus Christ as Savior: *"For God so loved the world, that he gave his only begotten Son, that whosoever believeth in him should not perish, but have everlasting life"* (John 3:16). Whosoever will! God respects our free will: *"He that believeth on the Son hath everlasting life: and he that believeth not the Son shall not see life; but the wrath of God abideth on him"* (John 3:36).

As a believer, you know that Jesus died for your sin. But how will others find the same redemption? Where do we begin? Salvation must start at home—with sons, daughters, spouses, and parents. Then we must reach out to our extended family members—uncles, aunts, cousins, and grandparents, and to all those we love. They may not believe immediately, neither will God ever force them to receive Him, but total recovery of your family is a scriptural principle that runs through the entire Bible. Claim it!

Four Vital Household Recovery Steps

Right now, you may be praying for a wayward son or daughter. Perhaps you are deeply concerned about the spiritual condition of your parents or your spouse. Here are four steps to recovering your household:

- **Develop your prayer life.** *"Then you will have your delight in the Almighty, And lift up your face to God. You will make your prayer to Him, He will hear you"* (Job 22:26–27, NKJV). Intercession is a vital part of your lost loved ones coming to salvation. When you pray, you can affect the eternal destiny of each family member.

- **Stand on God's Word.** *"Receive, please, instruction from His mouth, And lay up His words in your heart"* (Job 22:22, NKJV). Answer questions with, "The Bible says," and quote a scripture. Instead of offering your own opinion, rely on the authority of the Word. Again and again, Jesus said, *"It is written"* (Matthew 4:4, 7, 10). According to 2 Timothy 2:15, we are to make certain we are equipped to know what the Bible says about sin, satan, God, and salvation: *"Study to shew thyself approved unto God, a workman that needeth not to be ashamed, rightly dividing the word of truth."*

- **Exercise your spiritual authority.** As a result of following God's plan, *"You will also declare a thing, And it will be established for you; So light will shine on your ways"* (Job 22:28, NKJV).

- **Seek God's wisdom and purity.** As you seek to rescue those you love, God will allow your words to become powerful and give your life new strength: *"When men are cast down, then thou shalt say, There is lifting up; and he shall save the humble person. He shall deliver the island of the innocent: and it is delivered by the pureness of thine hands"* (Job 22:29–30). What a marvelous promise! God will give you the power to lift men up and help bring them salvation.

The answer to leading your family to Christ is on the way, and it begins with you! Go and tell! What does it take to win people to the Lord? Prayer plus witnessing.

You have been called to bring the message of salvation to your family. Paul declares: *"Share with me in the sufferings for the gospel according to the power of God, who has saved us and called us with a holy calling, not according to our works, but according to His own purpose and grace which was given to us in Christ Jesus before time began"* (2 Timothy 1:8–9, NKJV). Rejoice in that calling as you help break the chains and set your loved ones free!

When the Word is preached, the Holy Ghost convicts people of sin and they are drawn to Christ. The apostle Paul said, *"How then shall they call on Him in whom they have not believed? And how shall they believe in Him of whom they have not heard? And how shall they hear without a preacher?"* (Romans 10:14, NKJV). What a wonderful privilege and awesome responsibility we have to tell family and friends about Jesus Christ!

STAND AGAINST THE ENEMY'S TRAPS

Have you ever glanced heavenward while prayerfully interceding for a lost loved one's salvation, and whispered, "Lord, will my loved one ever know You? Will he (or she) ever surrender to Your love?"

Regardless of how long a loved one has evaded the gentle wooing of the Holy Spirit as you have called out his or her name in prayer, according to the promises contained in God's Word, your loved ones can be saved—every one of them!

Perhaps you're thinking, "But you don't know *my* loved ones. It would take a miracle for them to be saved!" It doesn't matter how hopeless your loved ones may seem or how long they have continued in their own way. All your loved ones can be saved, and I want to show you from God's Word how that can come about.

Before this incredible victory can be realized, however, we must first understand what hinders our loved ones from coming to faith in Jesus Christ. The Bible declares in 2 Corinthians 4:3–4: *"But if our gospel be hid, it is hid to them that are lost. In whom the god of this world hath blinded the minds of them which believe not; lest the light of the glorious gospel of Christ who is the image of God, should shine unto them."*

What happens when a loved one refuses to come to the Savior? It can be overwhelming, especially to a new believer. You love Jesus. You want others to experience the life-changing and miracle-working Gospel. Yet they seem completely unwilling to listen. It is as if they are blind to God's goodness.

According to the Bible, there are five major ways in which sinners are trapped:

- **They are bound to the world.** Paul wrote to the believers at Ephesus, *"And you He made alive, who were dead in trespasses and sins, in which you once walked according to the course of this world"* (Ephesians 2:1–2, NKJV). Sinners are slaves to everything the world offers, becoming addicted to materialism, entertainment, and a multitude of ungodly vices.

- **They are bound to the will of satan.** Workers of iniquity walk *"according to the prince of the power of the air, the spirit who now works in the sons of disobedience"* (verse 2, NKJV). Satan reigns supreme over the sinner, controlling his actions at any time and any place.

- **They are bound to the lust of the flesh.** As unbelievers, we *"had our conversation in times past in the lusts of our flesh"* (verse 3). What are the "lusts" to which Paul is referring? Money, pride, sex—whatever the flesh desires. Don't be surprised if your loved ones view these things from another perspective. They are ruled by a different spirit.

- **They are bound to the desires of the mind.** Sinners are *"fulfill-ing the desires of the flesh and of the mind"* (verse 3). I am sure you've met people whose minds have become their masters. They think, "I want this," and their body immediately responds. The thoughts of a believer, however, are governed by an entirely different set of principles. Why? Because *"we have the mind of Christ"* (1 Corinthians 2:16).

- **They are bound to the wrath of God.** Those living outside the ark of the Almighty *"were by nature the children of wrath"* (Ephesians 2:3). The Lord can never be pleased with the person who embraces evil. They are a great disappointment and the object of His scorn.

This scripture declares that the light of the Gospel is always shin-ing, but the god of this world has blinded the unbeliever's mind. The mind of the unbeliever has been cloaked with spiritual darkness by the god of this world, the devil. The Gospel light is hidden because satan has made it impossible for that person to see the truth.

Satan is a cruel master. Jesus said, *"Verily, verily, I say unto you, Whosoever committeth sin is the servant of sin"* (John 8:34). However, there is an answer. Jesus then declared, *"If the Son therefore shall make you free, ye shall be free indeed"* (verse 36).

To reach out to someone who is snared by these five traps, take authority over sin's curse. Pray that the spirit of the world that is in your loved ones will be bound. The Word declares,

> *Refrain your voice from weeping,*
> *And your eyes from tears;*
> *For your work shall be rewarded, says the LORD,*
> *And they shall come back from the land of the enemy.*

There is hope in your future, says the LORD,
That your children shall come back to their own border.
(Jeremiah 31:16–17, NKJV)

Scripture declares that we have power over satan and the forces of hell: *"Behold, I give unto you power to tread on serpents and scorpions, and over all the power of the enemy: and nothing shall by any means hurt you"* (Luke 10:19). Therefore, you also have power over this mind-blinding spirit that has deceived your lost loved ones. Once you begin to understand this authority, you will witness the salvation of all of your loved ones.

I mentioned my own testimony about coming to the Savior and then what happened in my family. I will never forget how I prayed and prayed, especially for my parents to come to know the Lord. I would go to my room, where I was all alone, and ask God to touch them. One night I was in my room praying, and the Lord spoke to me. It shook me from my head to my toes. He said, "Quit asking me to save your parents. Take your authority, and tell the devil to let them go."

My instant thought was, "Lord, I thought that was Your job." Then finally, I realized that it was up to me to obey what God told me to do. The Lord revealed something to me in that moment about authority in Christ that I never saw before as a Christian.

I was always begging, "Oh please, please, please God." Until finally the Lord said, "Do it! It is in your hands." I said, "Devil, in the name of Jesus, let my mother go." Suddenly the boldness of God came on me, and I sensed the anointing right in my room.

The power of God came on me, and for half an hour I commanded the devil to let go of my parents. Holy anger arose in me, and I penetrated the enemy's camp in prayer. I used the weapons of war that God has given us, and I claimed God's promise for my parents.

Another time I also remember praying specifically for my mother.

Some nights I would physically sweat for hours, agonizing over her soul. Finally, I cried out, "Lord, how do I rescue her from this bondage?"

I will never forget the answer!

"You don't rescue," He told me. "You pray, and I will rescue."

A short while later, Jesus appeared to my mother and said, "I am your Savior." Christ drew her to Himself. Through the Holy Spirit's convicting power, she was gloriously born again.

Why did the breakthrough occur? It came because I took my place in Christ Jesus and claimed the promises in God's Word for my parents. I did what I was supposed to do, then I turned it over to God. He did the rest. I will thank Him throughout eternity for what He did in my family.

The key is that I could not have taken my place had I not been in prayer. Then I began to understand the authority a believer has in Jesus Christ.

It is just like when Moses was on his face praying and God said, "Get up, and stretch the rod." At some point Moses had to act upon his faith in God if he wanted to see a miracle, and so did I. And so can you.

Prodigals in Your Family

The Bible is filled with so many examples of wayward loved ones coming back, perhaps none so well known as the prodigal son. The prodigal son is one of the best-known parables of Jesus. The story, found in Luke 15:11–32, refers to a son who returned home after squandering his fortune. In the story told by Jesus, a man had two sons. The younger demanded his share of his inheritance while his father is still living, and then he went off to a distant country where he wasted all the money with "riotous living."

What happened next should give hope to every prodigal son or daughter:

And when he came to himself, he said, How many hired servants of my father's have bread enough and to spare, and I perish with hunger! I will arise and go to my father, and will say unto him, Father, I have sinned against heaven, and before thee, And am no more worthy to be called thy son: make me as one of thy hired servants. And he arose, and came to his father. But when he was yet a great way off, his father saw him, and had compassion, and ran, and fell on his neck, and kissed him. And the son said unto him, Father, I have sinned against heaven, and in thy sight, and am no more worthy to be called thy son. But the father said to his servants, Bring forth the best robe, and put it on him; and put a ring on his hand, and shoes on his feet: And bring hither the fatted calf, and kill it; and let us eat, and be merry: For this my son was dead, and is alive again; he was lost, and is found. And they began to be merry. (Luke 15:17–24)

The story is traditionally referred to as "the prodigal son," but many argue that "the lost son" would be a more apt title, showing its parallels to the parables of the lost sheep and the lost coin, which immediately precede it in Luke 15. In all three the theme is the concern of God for the repenting sinner.

There is hope! Read that chapter over and over as you intercede for your family members. Your faith will be built as you claim that your loved ones will come back from enemy territory. You are breaking the strongholds of the world, satan's will, the lust of the flesh, the mind, and the wrath they are under.

Say, "Father, in the name of Jesus, because of the blood, I am asking you to loose them from the will of satan!" You can break the will of the devil, because *"greater is he that is in you, than he that is in the world"* (1 John 4:4).

A Final Note

Never give up hope! There is too much at stake. Thankfully though, we have a major role in the salvation of our household; we have a powerful ally in the Holy Spirit who quickens and convicts those who are lost.

The Bible clearly teaches us that the work of the Holy Spirit in a sinner's heart is necessary for salvation. The new birth comes about by God's sovereign work through the Holy Spirit: *"The wind bloweth where it listeth, and thou hearest the sound thereof, but canst not tell whence it cometh, and whither it goeth: so is every one that is born of the Spirit"* (John 3:8).

Revelation 3:20 describes God's persistent desire to draw the lost to Himself: *"Behold, I stand at the door, and knock: if any man hear my voice, and open the door, I will come in to him, and will sup with him, and he with me."*

God can work mightily in your family, too, as you pray and stand upon His Word. He will rescue. As you intercede and take authority, you will see the chains of darkness break.

Think of what can happen as each member of your family receives the Savior then becomes filled with the desire to seek to bring other loved ones to Jesus Christ. What a wonderful blessing to see God's multiplication power take over. Only heaven will reveal what can happen as you begin to see the Holy Spirit unleashed in your household.

Now is the time! Remember that God has offered salvation for you and your entire household. The Lord is asking you to stand in the gap for others. You can help break the chains and set your loved ones free.

Deuteronomy 7:9 says, *"Therefore know that the LORD your God, He is God, the faithful God who keeps covenant and mercy for a thousand generations with those who love Him and keep His commandments"* (NKJV). God is a covenant-keeping God. Because of that covenant, your loved ones can be saved.

Serve Him. Live the abundant life. Pray. God will rescue your household!

7

WEAPONS OF
TOTAL RECOVERY

*Who is this King of glory? The L*ORD *strong and mighty, the L*ORD *mighty in battle.*

—PSALM 24:8, NIV

T hroughout the Psalms, it is clear that those who believe in total recovery, those who act upon the Word of God, take the sword of the Spirit, and use it against the devil. Ephesians 4:27 says: *"Neither give place to the devil."* You are in authority, not him. When the Bible says to give no place to him, it puts the power in your hands by telling you not to let him in.

It is also apparent from David's life and writings that he understood the need to use specific weapons available to him. As a young man, he refused to wear ill-fitting armor and unproven weapons, even though he was going up against one of the most mighty warriors in history:

> *And it came to pass, when the Philistine arose, and came and drew nigh to meet David, that David hasted, and ran toward the army to meet the Philistine. And David put his hand in his bag, and took thence a stone, and slang it, and smote the Philistine in his forehead, that the stone sunk into his forehead;*

and he fell upon his face to the earth. So David prevailed over the Philistine with a sling and with a stone, and smote the Philistine, and slew him; but there was no sword in the hand of David. Therefore David ran, and stood upon the Philistine, and took his sword, and drew it out of the sheath thereof, and slew him, and cut off his head therewith. And when the Philistines saw their champion was dead, they fled. (1 Samuel 17:48–51)

In this story, David used two specific weapons, a sling and a stone. Throughout his life, David and those around him used many more weapons. In this book, we have discussed the weapons he and his 3-D army used to recover all: praise, prayer, pursuit, and power.

David wrote, *"Blessed be the LORD my strength, which teacheth my hands to war, and my fingers to fight"* (Psalm 144:1). He understood the weaponry of battle. He also understood that his land was surrounded by armies and rogue warriors who wanted to vanquish his people.

THE INVISIBLE BATTLEFIELD

We are at war! And the conflict in which we are engaged is unlike any warfare mankind can wage against humanity, for the forces to be reckoned with are more threatening than any natural force known and the stakes are eternal!

The Bible makes it clear that as believers this warfare involves a foe that is not of this world. Equipped with greater weaponry than the military might of any nation or international power, our enemy opposes us in the spirit realm in the battle of the ages.

Preparing for Battle

Identify the Enemy

First it is imperative to determine who your enemy really is and be spiritually prepared for battle. Preparation for spiritual warfare requires the application of spiritual principles revealed in the Word of God.

Never underestimate the capabilities of your adversary or the deceptiveness he will use in his attempt to defeat you: *"For we wrestle not against flesh and blood, but against principalities, against powers, against the rulers of the darkness of this world, against spiritual wickedness in high places"* (Ephesians 6:12). Satan does not fight alone. Let's quickly examine the five divisions of Satan's army mentioned in the verse above.

The five divisions in satan's army include:

1. **Spirits or demons**—the Word of God says, *"We wrestle not against flesh and blood."*
2. **Principalities**—from the Greek word *arche,* or "chief rulers of the highest rank."
3. **Powers**—from the Greek work *exousia,* or "authorities." These authorities operate the chief rulers, executing their will.
4. **Rulers of the darkness of this world**—world rulers of darkness; natural men possessing demonic powers. "This world" (*cosmos*) binds them to the natural and refers to governments or individuals in high authority in this world who are demon led or directed.
5. **Spiritual wickedness in high places**—wicked spirits in the heavens; fallen angels.

Be Strong in the Lord

Strength to subdue and defeat the enemy is not found in the natural; it is found in the Lord. The Bible commands us as believers to *"be strong in the Lord, and in the power of his might"* (Ephesians 6:10). The Greek word implies the command to "be strengthened" in Christ's might, as is promised to the believer: *"And what is the exceeding greatness of his power to us-ward who believe, according to the working of his mighty power"* (Ephesians 1:19).

Recognize who you are in Christ and acknowledge the real source of your strength. Don't attempt to fight the forces of hell alone, for the power to subdue and defeat the enemy does not rest in your strength; it comes from the Lord. Luke 10:19 declares: *"I give unto you power to tread on serpents and scorpions, and over all the power of the enemy: and nothing shall by any means hurt you."*

Clothe Yourself with the Armor of God

A prepared soldier will not go into battle without the appropriate armor. The potential for victory in a battle hinges upon suitable armor and appropriate weaponry. A spiritual battle requires spiritual weapons. It's impossible to avert the attacks of the devil and prevail against his strategies under your own strength. The Word of God instructs, *"Put on the whole armour of God, that ye may be able to stand against the wiles of the devil"* (Ephesians 6:11).

The Word of God continues on this theme stating, *"Wherefore, take unto you the whole armour of God, that ye may be able to withstand in the evil day and having done all, to stand"* (Ephesians 6:13). Subsequent scriptures describe essential armor and weaponry for the believer's use in withstanding and defeating the enemy. It is interesting to note that the first five pieces of armor have a defensive purpose while the remaining two pieces are for offense. Defensive armor provides protection for the vital organs of the soldier when facing the enemy in battle. From a spiritual perspective, the whole armor of God, applied and used properly, provides full protection and enables the believer to hold his ground against the enemy until victory comes.

ARMOR OF GOD

In Ephesians 6, Paul the apostle gives us the weapons necessary for a victorious Christian life. In order to be strong as a mighty overcomer and pursue total recovery, you must put on your armor.

"Loins girt about with truth"

Your mind is the first place you have to protect with the Word of God: *"Wherefore take unto you the whole armour of God, that ye may be able to withstand in the evil day, and having done all, to stand. Stand therefore, having your loins girt about with truth, and having on the breastplate of righteousness"* (Ephesians 6:13–14).

Your "loins" deal with your mind. We learn in 1 Peter 1:13 to "gird up the loins of your mind." Fill your mind with the Word, for the Spirit enters the door of the mind.

"The breastplate of righteousness"

The second weapon you must have is the breastplate of righteousness (Ephesians 6:14). The breastplate covers a soldier's vital organs and speaks of the heart. The breastplate of righteousness fortifies the heart against the attacks of the enemy. Allow the righteousness revealed in God's Word to influence your mind and touch your heart.

When the truth of God's Word touches your mind and heart, it brings transformation and renewal: *"And be not conformed to this world: but be ye transformed by the renewing of your mind, that ye may prove what is that good, an acceptable, and perfect, will of God"* (Romans 12:2).

David, writing under the inspiration of the Holy Spirit, told us that we protect the heart by filling it with God's Word: *"Thy word have I hid in mine heart, that I might not sin against thee"* (Psalm 119:11).

Then we are to meditate upon what we have read:

> *Blessed is the man that walketh not in the counsel of the ungodly, nor standeth in the way of sinners, nor sitteth in the seat of the scornful. But his delight is in the law of the LORD; and in his law doth he meditate day and night. And he shall be like a tree planted by the rivers of water, that bringeth forth his fruit in his season; his leaf also shall not wither; and whatsoever he doeth shall prosper.* (Psalm 1:1–3)

Meditation is simply rehearsing to yourself what God has said in His Word. Meditation is a wonderful exercise where you can enjoy and digest the Word of God so that it affects your entire life and permeates deep into your heart. Once the Word of God is in your heart, it will protect you.

"Feet shod with the preparation of the gospel of peace"

Third, you must have *"your feet shod"* (Ephesians 6:15). As you shod your feet, you are protecting your life and your behavior. Every day the Word of God goes forth to touch and change the lives of people all around the world. Make sure you are one of them and that you carry His good news.

The Word of God must affect your life's walk. This happens as the Word fills your mind, touches your heart, and is manifested, or seen, in your walk. It all begins with your mind. You begin to read the Word and hear the Word; it begins to influence and fill your heart with truth. This affects your actions and in your daily life.

"The shield of faith"

The fourth weapon is faith: *"Above all, taking the shield of faith, where-with ye shall be able to quench all the fiery darts of the wicked"* (Ephesians 6:16). The Word in your mouth is faith. God's Word will pour forth out of your spirit and touch your speech, enabling you to stand strong against the enemy.

Faith brings powerful results, for when faith is joined with the results of the Word in your mind, heart, and life, we can withstand the onslaught of the enemy and render his fiery darts ineffective.

"The helmet of salvation"

Fifth, the helmet of salvation will guard your life: *"And take the helmet of salvation"* (Ephesians 6:17). In the natural the helmet protects the head from injury in battle. Some mistakenly believe that the helmet deals with the mind. However, the helmet of salvation deals with doctrine. That does not mean you wear a helmet like a soldier and protect your skull from a bullet; it means you protect your life from error.

Once the truth enters your mind, touches your heart, affects your life and walk, and is manifested in your actions, it becomes your nature. The helmet of salvation deals with your nature, your character, your doctrine. What you believe is who you are. The doctrine of the Word makes you balanced and stable. You are not moved by error or taken by false teaching. The helmet of salvation is the doctrine of the Word that brings balance to your life and keeps you walking steady and balanced with the Spirit and in the Spirit.

The Word of God will keep you on solid footing: *"That we hence-forth be no more children, tossed to and fro, and carried about with every wind of doctrine, by the sleight of men, and cunning craftiness, whereby they lie in wait to deceive"* (Ephesians 4:14).

Paul wrote of absolute necessity of God's Word to help you when faced with spiritual warfare:

> *Persecutions, afflictions, which came unto me at Antioch, at Iconium, at Lystra; what persecutions I endured: but out of them all the Lord delivered me. Yea, and all that will live godly in Christ Jesus shall suffer persecution. But evil men and seducers shall wax worse and worse, deceiving, and being deceived. But continue thou in the things which thou hast learned and hast been assured of, knowing of whom thou hast learned them; And that from a child thou hast known the holy scriptures, which are able to make thee wise unto salvation through faith which is in Christ Jesus. All scripture is given by inspiration of God, and is profitable for doctrine, for reproof, for correction, for instruction in righteousness: That the man of God may be perfect, thoroughly furnished unto all good works.* (2 Timothy 3:11–17)

The Word of God will affect your doctrine and when it does, balance will come to your life so that you are not easily swayed or taken away from the truth. This foundation is very important. It will help protect you against pollution and deception. He said, *"Take heed that no man deceive you"* (Matthew 24:4). It is your job to make sure that you are balanced. The Word of God interprets the Word of God. That means the Word explains the Word, so do not just go by one verse. Doctrine is built on more than a single verse.

"The sword of the Spirit"

The sixth weapon or piece of armor is *"the sword of the Spirit, which is the word of God"* (Ephesians 6:17). The Word of God in you becomes your weapon against the devil. No enemy can bring you down when you are full of God's Word.

All the armor up to this point has served a defensive purpose, intended for use in facing the enemy. Each piece of armor provided protection from an attack. And although the Word of God is connected to each element of God's armor, the sword of the Spirit is the Word of God, for it is used as an offensive weapon against the enemy.

The Word of God is an eternally potent weapon. The apostle Paul even uses weaponry terminology concerning the Bible: *"Study to shew thyself approved unto God, a workman that needeth not to be ashamed, rightly dividing the word of truth"* (2 Timothy 2:15).

The Word of God protects you against the enemy, affecting your mind, your heart, your walk, your actions, and your nature, character, and life. As your life becomes strong and established, the sword of the Spirit becomes an offensive weapon against the enemy. Unmovable, unshakable, and because of the truth within, you are able to stand against the enemy. When you become a masterful "swordsman," God can use you more than ever before in any total recovery battle!

In three consecutive instances Jesus Christ Himself used the Word of God as He resisted satan's temptation, saying, *"It is written..."* (Matthew 4:4–7). Armed with the sword of the Spirit, you can take back the territory that belongs to you, including your family, your finances, and your health, because you've strengthened yourself in the Spirit.

"Prayer and supplication"

The seventh and most important of all weapons is prayer. It is what keeps you. Over and over in this book I have referred to the absolute need for prayer, the prayer that covers and clothes you like a mantle.

It is impossible to effectively use the Word without prayer. Ephesians 6:18 encourages you to be a mighty person of prayer: *"Praying always with all prayer and supplication in the Spirit, and watching thereunto with all perseverance and supplication for all saints."*

E. M. Bounds said this about prayer:

This intense conflict with the devil requires sleepless vigilance, midnight vigils, and a wakefulness that cannot be surprised. It also requires a perseverance that knows neither halting, fainting, nor depression. This kind of praying knows by clear spiritual intelligence what it needs. The prayer warrior knows the unlimited provisions that are available to supply all his needs. He knows the necessity of perseverance in prayer until the need is supplied and provision is secured.[1]

Seven pieces of armor—seven weapons of war. Spiritual warfare is a reality for the believer, and the stakes involved in the conflict are eternal! According to Scripture, this struggle is not against *"flesh and blood, but against principalities, against powers, against the rulers of the darkness of this world, against spiritual wickedness in high places"* (Ephesians 6:12).

Preparation for spiritual warfare requires the application of spiritual principles revealed in the Word of God. As believers, we need never face the enemy in our own strength. David undoubtedly taught his own 3-D army these words:

> *It is God that girdeth me with strength, and maketh my way perfect. He maketh my feet like hinds' feet.... He teacheth my hands to war, so that a bow of steel is broken by mine arms. Thou hast also given me the shield of thy salvation.... I have pursued mine enemies, and overtaken them.... I have wounded them that they were not able to rise: they are fallen under my feet. For thou hast girded me with strength unto the battle.* (Psalm 18:32–39)

Regarding spiritual warfare, I have often cautioned, don't trust in your own strength or abilities, for the flesh is powerless and without authority against the enemy: *"Through God we shall do valiantly: for he it is that shall tread down our enemies"* (Psalm 60:12; 108:13).

All the armor and weaponry necessary to defeat your foe is available to you. Take time to identify your enemy, put on the whole armor of God, and clothe yourself with a mantle of prayer. When you are Spirit led and properly prepared in the realm of the Spirit, you will bring defeat to the enemy and victory to your life!

Angelic Forces Standing with You

Every believer will face spiritual battles. Since the Garden of Eden, satan has sought to enslave mankind and hold each of us captive.

The conflict in which we are engaged is not of this world. This battle is in the realm of the spirit! Spiritual battles are won spiritually. Thankfully, we have a full arsenal of weaponry. We also have to combat satan's evil forces. The angelic host of heaven stands ready to respond, and when you pray, the forces of the enemy will be destroyed. Notice how many different angelic forces are prepared to take action.

Seraphims. These heavenly beings are connected to God's glory. Isaiah 6:1–3 declares:

> *In the year that king Uzziah died I saw also the LORD sitting upon a throne, high and lifted up, and his train [skirt] filled the temple. Above it stood the seraphims: each one had six wings; with twain he covered his face, and with twain he covered feet, and with twain he did fly. And one cried unto another, and said, Holy, holy, holy, is the LORD of hosts: the whole earth is full of his glory.*

God's glory deals with His attributes and who He is. In response to God's inexhaustible revelation of Himself, the seraphims continually cry, *"Holy, holy, holy, is the LORD of hosts: the whole earth is full of his glory"* to one another. Because God's attributes are endless, each revelation prompts another response by an innumerable number of seraphims as they acknowledge His holiness.

Cherubims. These angelic beings are connected to worship and heaven, protectors of the throne of God. Hebrews 9:5 points to *"the cherubims of glory."* The presence and glory of God is so holy that the cherubims protect it, for it is the dwelling place of God.

Cherubims are in the holy presence of God continually, affecting their very appearance: *"And they sparkled like the colour of burnished brass"* (Ezekiel 1:7). They are involved in the work of the Spirit in heaven and what is happening in glory. These magnificent beings were worshiping God and protecting the throne of heaven.

Living Creatures. These are angels of revelation, revealing who God is to the heavens through exaltation and worship. Revelation 4 illuminates these angelic forces:

> *And, behold, a throne was set in heaven, and one sat on the throne. . . . And before the throne there was a sea of glass like unto crystal: and in the midst of the throne, and round about the throne, were four beasts full of eyes before and behind. The first beast was like a lion, and the second beast like a calf, and the third beast had a face as a man, and the fourth beast was like a flying eagle. And four beasts had each of them, the word of God says, they had six wings about him; and they were full of eyes within: and they rest not day and night, saying, Holy, holy, holy, Lord God Almighty, which was, and is, and is to come. And when those beasts give glory and honour and thanks to him that sat on the throne, who liveth for ever and ever.* (Revelation 4:2, 6–9)

While the seraphims acknowledge the holiness of God to one another in worship and adoration, these angels are found before the throne crying, *"Holy, holy, holy, LORD God Almighty, which was, and is, and is to come"* to God Himself.

Archangels. These messengers or ministers are involved in the affairs of men. The archangel announced Christ's birth: *"Behold, I bring you good tidings of great joy, which shall be to all people. For unto you is born this day in the city of David a Savior, which is Christ the Lord"* (Luke 2:10–11). They will also foretell His second coming: *"For the Lord himself shall descend from heaven with a shout, with the voice of the archangel, and with the trump of God"* (1 Thessalonians 4:16).

They are involved in spiritual warfare and protection: *"But the prince of the kingdom of Persia withstood me one and twenty days; but, lo, Michael, one of the chief princes, came to help me"* (Daniel 10:13).

They stand in God's presence: *"And the angel answering said unto him, I am Gabriel, that stand in the presence of God; and am sent to speak unto thee"* (Luke 1:19).

Angels. These heavenly beings are dispatched through prayer. There are 300 references to angels in the Bible, suggesting the importance God places on this subject.

Here are a few examples:

- Angels are wise and aware of events on earth: *"According to the wisdom of an angel of God, to know all things that are in the earth"* (2 Samuel 14:20).
- Angels are powerful: *"And after these things I saw another angel come down from heaven, having great power"* (Revelation 18:1).
- Angels are obedient: *"Bless the LORD, ye his angels that excel in strength, that do his commandments, hearkening unto the voice of his*

word. Bless ye the LORD, all ye his hosts, ye ministers of his that do his pleasure" (Psalm 103:20–21).

- Angels strengthen us in times of trial, as one strengthened Jesus on the Mount of Olives before His betrayal: *"And there appeared an angel unto him from heaven, strengthening him"* (Luke 22:43).
- Angels protect the saints: *"The angel of the LORD encampeth round about them that fear him, and delivereth them"* (Psalm 34:7).
- Angels bring clarity and understanding to the will of God: *"There was a certain man in Caesarea called Cornelius, a centurion of the band called the Italian band. A devout man and one that feared God…which gave much alms…and prayed to God always. He saw in a vision…an angel of God coming to him and saying unto him, Cornelius. And he looked on him and he was afraid, and said, What is it Lord? And he said unto him, Thy prayers and thine alms are come up for a memorial before God. And now send men to Joppa, and call for one Simon, whose surname is Peter: He lodgeth with one Simon a tanner, whose house is by the seaside: he shall tell thee what thou oughtest to do"* (Acts 10:1–6).
- Angels are without number, innumerable: *"I beheld till the thrones were cast down, and the Ancient of days did sit, whose garment was white as snow, and the hair of his head like the pure wool: his throne was like the fiery flame, and his wheels as burning fire. A fiery stream issued and came forth from before him: thousand thousands ministered unto him, and ten thousand times ten thousand stood before him: the judgment was set, and the books were opened"* (Daniel 7:9–10).

Understanding what we know about David and what happened to his 3-D army, is it any wonder why there are so many references to angelic forces throughout the Psalms? We should take heart. Those same angelic forces are available to us today!

Remember, as a believer, you need never face the enemy in your own strength. As David encouraged us:

> *It is God that girdeth me with strength, and maketh my way perfect. He maketh my feet like hinds' feet.... He teacheth my hands to war, so that a bow of steel is broken by mine arms. Thou hast given me the shield of thy salvation.... I have pursued mine enemies, and overtaken them.... I have wounded them that they were not able to rise: they are fallen under my feet. For thou hast girded me with strength unto the battle.* (Psalm 18:32–39)

In faith—through praise, prayer, pursuit, and power—you can tear down the strongholds of the enemy. The devil trembles when a believer understands these principles of total recovery. As a believer, you can bring defeat to the forces of hell.

Take your position on the battlefield starting today. Sound the battle cry! The hosts of heaven stand ready for battle as a mighty army. Be persistent and don't give up. The battle is already won. Victory is on the way!

SPIRITUAL VICTORY

When you resist the devil, James 4:7 says, *"He will flee from you."* It is time that Christians come against the enemy and say, "In the name of Jesus, no devil, you cannot have my family, you cannot touch my finances, and you cannot put sickness upon me!"

At Holy Spirit Miracle Crusades all over the world, that is exactly what my staff, my intercessory army, and I do. We come offensively against the devil to let God's people go. Then we come offensively against the spirit of sickness and bondage that has held God's people for too long. When a believer claims authority and breaks the power of the enemy in the name of Jesus Christ, bound people will be set free.

Jesus has already won your victory on the cross, so all you must do is enforce His victory by walking in your God-given authority and demand the devil to let go. None of us would have this mighty authority without Jesus. We cannot fight in our own names.

We must enforce Christ's authority by taking His place on earth and proclaiming liberty to the oppressed, the sick, and those who are bound in Jesus's name. Psalm 149:6–7 says, *"Let the high praises of God be in their mouth, and a twoedged sword in their hand; to execute vengeance."*

I have news for you: The evil forces we fight in those crusades are the same forces that try to destroy you and your loved ones. What are you doing about them? Are you taking your authority in Jesus and coming against them? We are told in 1 Peter 5:8 to *"Be sober, be vigilant; because your adversary the devil, as a roaring lion, walketh about, seeking whom he may devour."*

You have power over all the power of the enemy, and he is under your feet. That is how you recover all!

TAKING THE OFFENSIVE

Defense is good, but we must also learn to take the offensive strategy. The church must quit looking around and wondering where the devil will attack next. He is the one who should be wondering where you will attack next. The church is the one moving ahead against him, not the other way around.

You have nothing to fear in battle. As David and his 3-D army proved, once and for all, He carries you and holds you up. God thrusts out your enemies from before you. He is your refuge in the time of battle, and you can find rest in His care.

Deuteronomy 33:27 commands: *"The eternal God is thy refuge, and underneath are the everlasting arms: and he shall thrust out the enemy from before thee."* The commandment from heaven given in the book of Deuteronomy is very clear: God's will is for you to destroy the enemy. In other words, do not let him destroy you; you must go first and destroy him. That is how you fight on the offense.

Though warfare can make you weary, God will cause you to dwell in safety, and He will lead you to a refreshing place where fountains are upon the land. God will cause the heavens to drop down dew on you and He will be the sword of your excellency.

As you fight on the offense and demonstrate faith in the victory Christ won on the cross, you are telling the devil that he has already been defeated and the battle has already been won.

The church is engaged in a war, and you cannot be victorious if you do not accept your place as a conquering soldier and fight. It is every Christian's job to be a soldier of the kingdom of God—a soldier of the cross.

E. M. Bounds said:

> We are not imaginary soldiers fighting an imaginary war—all is real and true. Because he is truthful, a girded soldier is strong, prepared, and intense in his fight. Truth is the ornament of a jeweled belt, a diamond set in gold. We must conquer the devil by truth as the strength and support of our lives. We know the truth and have the truth because we have Christ who is the truth.[2]

It is vital to your success in this life as a Christian, especially as you learn to use the principles of total recovery, that you lay aside the cares of this world and keep heaven's purpose on your mind. In 2 Timothy 2:4

we learn: *"No man that warreth entangleth himself with the affairs of this life; that he may please him who hath chosen him to be a soldier."*

You have been chosen to be a part of God's holy army. In order to fight the good fight you must lay aside the weights that hold you back from total recovery.

Fear, for example, is a strong weight that will hold you back if you let it. We must come out and fight in faith rather than hide in fear. God's Word says, *"For God hath not given us the spirit of fear; but of power, and of love, and of a sound mind"* (2 Timothy 1:7).

God has promised you power to subdue your enemies and recover your losses. You can read Revelation and know how the war ends, even before it is fought!

Revelation 17:14 shares: *"These shall make war with the Lamb, and the Lamb shall overcome them: for he is Lord of lords, and King of kings: and they that are with him are called, and chosen, and faithful."*

God has already made you an overcomer, so do not hide or be reluctant to battle because of fear. Those who are full of faith and believe activate God's promises for total recovery.

GOD-GIVEN POWER

To have total recovery, you must know what belongs to you and its value, or otherwise you may never do a thing about recovering it. Recovery cannot happen if you sit and wait for it to happen. Recovery comes to you when you pursue your enemy and attack him. Many dear Christians sit and wait, hoping for recovery to come to them, and in the meantime the enemy continues to steal from them.

In order to have total recovery, you must know that your power is greater than your enemy's. *Power* translates as "delegated authority" in the Greek. It is like a police officer who has the authority to stop a car;

he can stop the car because he has been given the authority to do it. The authority that God has given you operates the same way.

As you pursue your enemy, the devil will recognize the power that has been given to you. The problem is that many Christians do not recognize or walk in the authority and power that they have been given.

You can stop the enemy and take back what belongs to you today. Daniel 11:32 says, *"But the people that do know their God shall be strong, and do exploits."* God's power is a clear promise from heaven, and the moment you stand in faith upon that promise is the moment you can face the enemy without fear and recover all.

The Lord is looking for the one who will rise up, stand up for Him, and be a man or woman of total recovery. Psalm 94:16 says, *"Who will rise up for me against the evildoers? or who will stand up for me against the workers of iniquity?"*

When I stand in the great crusade arenas under the anointing of the Holy Spirit and say, "In the name of Jesus let this person go," people often say they felt warmth like electricity flow through them. What do you think is happening in that moment? That is God's promise from Psalm 107:16 being fulfilled: *"He hath broken the gates of brass, and cut the bars of iron in sunder."* The gates here are symbolic of a place of power and of bondage, but God's Word declares that you have power over the enemy who brings bondage.

For example, if a demonic spirit oppresses someone or they are under the control of an evil spirit, you can pray in the name of Jesus and see that person released from the power holding them. Jesus said that in His name we will cast out devils. You have authority in Jesus's name to see strongholds released and your loved ones set free from demonic influence.

God has given you mighty weapons to set yourself and others free. You must simply act upon your faith and declare God's Word in your own situation, in your home, and over your loved ones. We learn in

2 Corinthians 10:4: *"For the weapons of our warfare are not carnal, but mighty through God to the pulling down of strong holds."*

THE NAME OF JESUS CHRIST

The name of Jesus is a weapon against the enemy because there is power in the name of Jesus. You would not be a Christian if you did not believe there is power in Jesus's name, so continue to stand upon the name of Jesus to battle as you pray. The name of Jesus has power against any devil that harasses you.

The blood of Jesus is another offensive weapon against the enemy because it has power to protect and keep you. You overcome by the blood of the Lamb and the word of your testimony. The two go hand in hand. The blood is not effective without the spoken word.

Jesus used the spoken word of God in the wilderness when the devil came to tempt Him. He said, "It is written, it is written, it is written." The Lord Jesus stands victorious against the devil, and you will too as you stand on His name, proclaim the power of the blood, and speak the Word of God.

I learned a valuable lesson about the power of the spoken word at one of my meetings in Toronto, Canada. A woman came forward for prayer and I laid my hand on her to pray for her, yet nothing happened to her. I prayed three times and still nothing happened.

I thought, "Lord, nothing is happening, but still I feel the presence of Your anointing all over me. Your presence is in this building, so why isn't this lady receiving?"

He said, "Say the words." I thought, "What have my words got to do with it?" I was laying hands on the people who came up for prayer, but nothing was happening. This continued throughout the whole service until finally I laid hands on someone and said the words, "The power of God goes through you."

Wham! Instantly, God touched the person. The Lord was teaching me something very important that you must understand too. The power of God flows through your words.

You must speak the word of faith to see the results of your prayers. You will see tremendous results as you speak God's Word, God's promises, and God's blessings over your life and the lives of your loved ones.

A Final Note

Is there something you have prayed and prayed for and yet have seen no results? You will see recovery and restoration come when you pray for that situation or that loved one under the anointing of the Holy Ghost and take your authority in Christ.

With the authority that God has given you, you stop asking and start commanding the enemy to release what belongs to you. Faith-filled prayers activate heaven's answer.

Whatever situation you are facing in your home or family today can be lifted to the Lord in prayer. God has given you the authority to combat your enemies with Jesus's name, the blood of the Cross, and the spoken Word of God.

Why not fight offensively today with these weapons of war? The Lord's promise to you is that as you are built up to fight, you can march against the enemy, and now power will stand with you.

Like David, you can march in and recover all that has been stolen from you. What God has given you is yours; you have a legal right to it, and God wants you to get it back!

8

YOUR ANOINTING FOR
TOTAL RECOVERY

Thou anointest my head with oil; my cup runneth over. Surely goodness and mercy shall follow me all the days of my life: and I will dwell in the house of the LORD for ever.

—PSALM 23:5–6

One of the greatest reasons for David's total recovery is that he was sustained by God's anointing upon his life. That anointing started long before David began rebuilding his tattered 3-D army. Let's look backward a few years.

I have often reflected upon the scene written of in 1 Samuel 16, the day that Samuel anointed David. I can only imagine that Samuel's mission was clear. The Lord had spoken to him regarding the sons of Jesse. One of them would be anointed king, and God was going to show him which of Jesse's sons to anoint.

Samuel most likely wasted no time as his purposeful eyes looked up and down at each of Jesse's sons. Jesse may have said, "Step forward Abinadab and let Samuel see you." While Samuel's eyes questioned the young man, he was mindful that God does not judge by outward appearance but looks at a man's thoughts and intentions. "This is not the right man," Samuel may have declared as Jesse summoned several of his other sons to step forward, only to hear Samuel say, "These are not the right men either."

In the same way, all seven of Jesse's sons presented themselves to Samuel and each was rejected. "The Lord has not chosen any of them," Samuel told Jesse while turning to look around to make sure he had seen them all.

"Are these all there are?" Samuel asked. Jesse, most likely taken aback by Samuel's question, remembered his youngest son. "W-W-Well . . . there is my youngest son, David," Jesse might have muttered, "but he is out in the fields watching the sheep."

"Send for him at once," Samuel said, "for we will not sit down to eat until he arrives." I can imagine how with surprise Jesse immediately sent for David.

Can you imagine how David must have felt when he heard that Samuel the prophet was asking to see him? David's heart must have leaped as he jumped up from the place where he was sitting, attending to the sheep. I can imagine David running swiftly to meet them.

Most likely panting, breathless from the run, David stood humbly before Samuel the prophet, his father Jesse, and his brothers. I have thought about how Samuel's expression must have changed as a light came to his wide eyes seeing the young man who stood before him. Samuel looked upon David, noticing he was a fine looking boy with a ruddy face and pleasant eyes. Just then the Lord spoke to Samuel and said, "This is the one; anoint him." I can see David, his head bowed with hands folded in front of him, expressing utmost reverence to Samuel and the word of the Lord.

As David stood among his brothers, Samuel took the olive oil he had brought and poured it upon David's head. In those moments, oil would have flowed down David's strong cheeks as tears filled his understanding eyes. It doesn't take much imagination to think how David might have acknowledged the anointing that had come upon him with a deep, infilling breath. And throughout the land, it was known that from that day forward, the Spirit of Jehovah gave David great power.

DAVID'S PREPARATION

Can you imagine how David's personal time with God exploded after that life-changing day? In fact, in order to understand God's anointing for your life, it is beneficial to learn from biblical example. David had three anointings.

The first, just discussed, took place when Samuel went to see David's father, Jesse, and anointed David. David's first anointing did not change his duties; he continued toiling in the fields then was called on occasion to play the harp for Saul.

David's second anointing followed the conflict with the house of Saul after the king's death.

Only after David's third anointing did he have dominion and authority over all of Israel. To reach the level of dominion and authority that God intends for your life, you must receive the fullness of God's anointing. I call it "the kingly anointing."

In much the same way, the apostles experienced three anointings. Their anointing first came when Jesus breathed on them and said, *"Receive ye the Holy Ghost"* (John 20:22). Their second anointing came upon them when the Holy Spirit fell on them on the Day of Pentecost (Acts 2). Finally, the third anointing came as they spoke *"the Word of God with boldness"* (Acts 4:31).

A greater anointing will come upon you as you continue to abide in the Lord. The same great power and anointing that came upon David can pour out upon your life.

Smith Wigglesworth, a great evangelist of the early 1900s and a man who knew the power of God's anointing said:

> It is not sufficient just to have a touch of God or to usually have a desire for God. There is only one thing that will meet the needs of the people today, and that is to be immersed in the life of God—God taking you and filling you with His Spirit, until you live right in God, and God lives in you, so that *"whether you eat or drink, or whatever you do,"* it will all be for the *"glory of God."* (1 Corinthians 10:31)[1]

As Smith Wigglesworth described, are you hungry to be filled with God's Spirit? Are you ready to recover all as you move into an entirely new dimension of God's power? God wants you to be immersed in His anointing today.

Did you know that there is a unique anointing of God on every believer? God's Word tells us that *"he which stablisheth us…hath anointed us"* (2 Corinthians 1:21). The Bible says, *"He which….hath anointed us, is God."* God's power and anointing are available to you today.

Special Anointing for Special Times

Just as David's anointing was given to prepare him for the historic times he faced, I believe we are being given a special anointing for the amazing days ahead. In fact, I believe fire is going to fall on God's people in the last days. The Bible clearly shows that God is about to pour His Spirit out on all flesh. The book of Joel promises: *"And it shall come to pass afterward, that I will pour out my spirit upon all flesh; and your sons and your daughters shall prophesy, your old men shall dream dreams, your young men shall see visions"* (Joel 2:28).

God's Word brings His anointing upon your life. In the book of Numbers, the people ate manna that tasted like oil. Today, the Word of the living God is the manna that brings the anointing on your life:

> *And the manna was as coriander seed, and the colour thereof as the colour of bdellium. And the people went about, and gathered it, and ground it in mills, or beat it in a mortar, and baked it in pans, and made cakes of it: and the taste of it was as the taste of fresh oil. And when the dew fell upon the camp in the night, the manna fell upon it.* (Numbers 11:7–9)

The time is coming when God's glory will fall on congregations before the church service even begins. The Word of God, or fresh manna, will be filled with a heavy anointing. This anointing, coming upon the lives of God's people, will descend in great power.

Isaiah 10:27 contains a mighty promise of God dealing with the anointing that you can claim as you read this book: *"And it shall come to pass in that day, that his burden shall be taken away from off thy shoulder, and his yoke from off thy neck, and the yoke shall be destroyed because of the anointing."*

David understood the power of the anointing of the Spirit. The anointing is evident throughout the Psalms. *"Thou anointest my head with oil; my cup runneth over. Surely goodness and mercy shall follow me all the days of my life: and I will dwell in the house of the LORD for ever"* (Psalm 23:5–6). That same anointing of the Lord has power to set you free, to help you recover all, and to bring you into the fullness of God.

Peter experienced God's fullness in his life as the anointing brought about a supernatural manifestation of God through him. So much so, in fact, that Peter's own shadow raised the dead. Can you imagine an anointing of God upon your life like that? The Lord wants you to walk so closely with Him that even your shadow carries His presence, as Peter's shadow did.

Throughout history, men and women of great faith in God have experienced this powerful anointing. Charles Finney was most certainly one of them. Books record from Finney's day how he often preached in a packed building where thousands more waited outside. Sometimes more were outside than were able to get inside, with people healed both inside and outside the building.

Just the very fact that they were in the same area as Finney enabled them to receive God's healing touch. People who knew nothing about the meeting and had no interest in God would come under conviction, crumble, and confess their sins, simply by passing by the building where Finney ministered. That is what the power of the anointing of God will do in a person's life who is yielded to Him.

SEARCHING FOR THE ANOINTING

After I became a believer, I began searching for God's presence in a greater way in my life. I heard many evangelists, ministers, and teachers talk about the infilling of the Holy Spirit, but none of them spoke of the Holy Spirit as Kathryn Kuhlman did.

She spoke of a Person who was real and alive. She often pointed her finger down at the crowd and said, "He's more real to me than you, more real than anything in this world!"

I can remember reflecting upon Kathryn's words as I lay stretched out on my bed one night in Toronto. Every bone in my body was aching for sleep, yet my eyes were wide open thinking about the Holy Spirit that Miss Kuhlman described.

In that dark room, I knew God was at work, and I was more than ready to follow His leading. My heart was filled with questions, and I didn't quite know where to begin. I wondered, "How can I have what that evangelist in Pittsburgh had experienced?" I had developed a hunger, a craving to know the Holy Spirit in that same dimension. Yet I did not know where to begin.

Something penetrated deep inside me and I cried and said, "Lord, please let me know You like this." The Holy Spirit immediately began revealing Himself to me, bringing His anointing upon my life. He will make Himself known to you, and you will see the results of His presence in your life, too, as you call upon Him and ask Him to come and fill you.

As with the 3-D army, you must desire to go beyond where you are now. The Christian life is a process of growth. If there is no growth, it is because there is death, or a lack of fresh fellowship in your life. Growth is a natural and supernatural part of life. The moment you begin life in Christ, God promised that His anointing upon you would intensify.

- The anointing that came on you when you were saved is the first level of God's anointing. God first brings His presence to cleanse and save you: *"And the remnant of the oil that is in the priest's hand he shall pour upon the head of him that is to be cleansed: and the priest shall make an atonement for him before the LORD"* (Leviticus 14:18).

- The next anointing is the anointing that brings you into ministry. This anointing enables you to serve God: *"And thou shalt anoint Aaron and his sons, and consecrate them, that they may minister unto me in the priest's office"* (Exodus 30:30).

- Then the anointing upon your life will bring authority. David came into authority because of the anointing upon him: *"So all the elders of Israel came to the king to Hebron; and king David made a league with them in Hebron before the LORD: and they anointed David king over Israel"* (2 Samuel 5:3).

The minute you are born again, God asks, "Do you want any more? Will you go deeper? Will you come closer?" As you surrender your life to God, the Holy Spirit moves into new levels of the anointing of God.

Some dear Christians have wondered, "Why don't I have a greater anointing?" It is not that God is not giving it; they are simply not opening to receive it. You receive by opening your heart to God, surrendering, and allowing Him to fill you. All that you must do is surrender. It does not cost a thing; Christ Jesus has already paid the price.

TOTAL RECOVERY AND THE ANOINTING

The Holy Spirit is being poured out on the church, and bondages are being broken. Victories are being won. Total recovery is happening. Everywhere I travel I am amazed to see what God is doing.

The Holy Spirit is being poured out on this generation! The anointing of God brings liberty and the miraculous to the lives of God's people. Isaiah 10:27 testifies of this truth: "*And it shall come to pass in that day, that his burden shall be taken away from off thy shoulder, and his yoke from off thy neck, and the yoke shall be destroyed because of the anointing.*"

The word *destroyed* in this passage gives the picture of something turning into dust and blowing away in the wind. In Hebrew, the word *destroyed* goes a step further, and even gives the picture of something that is totally forgotten.

The anointing destroys the misery you have experienced because of satan's power. The anointing shatters the yoke of sin that has bound you, and once the anointing destroys it, it will never be remembered or seen again.

Somebody may ask you, "Do you remember your old life? Do you remember the way you were?"

Most believers who have known the anointing will say, "I don't even think about it."

Why is that? Simple! The very thought of the old man is not even there. The anointing that breaks the yoke destroys the bondages of yesterday, so much so that you do not even think about the past anymore.

Once you become a new creation in Christ, you identify less and less with your old self. The moment you came into Christ by asking Jesus to forgive your sins and come into your heart, you were born again and the liberty of God became yours. The anointing destroys the yoke of bondage.

True believers are not living in the bondage they lived in before Christ Jesus came in. John 8:36 declares, *"If the Son therefore shall make you free, ye shall be free indeed."* Old things are passed away.

Total recovery can be yours. Yes, we still live in bodies that will corrupt. We have not yet put on immortality so we must still fight sin. The difference is that once we are born again, we are no longer in bondage or slavery to sin. Thank God for the blood of Christ, our cleansing fountain!

In fact, the anointing can be described as a river that flows from deep within: *"And it shall come to pass, that every thing that liveth, which moveth, whithersoever the rivers shall come, shall live…every thing shall live whither the river cometh"* (Ezekiel 47:9).

God pours His Spirit out to bring life in such a way for a specific reason. He is not pouring it so your emotions can tingle. The anointing descends for a higher purpose than an emotional experience. God wants to fill you with His life, and through you fill someone else with His life, and in turn reach the world.

God desires you to walk into a deeper level, a higher dimension in Him. It is all yours, if you want it. In the book of 2 Samuel, David moved into that authority and it brought fullness to him. Scripture says that the fullness of the anointing belongs to you: *"But ye are come unto mount Sion, and unto the city of the living God"* (Hebrews 12:22).

Someone once asked me, "Where do you go from here?" I said, "Higher." Eternity never stops. God's blessing and anointing is without measure, and that is why the Christian life is so exciting. You will never come to the end of your experience in God. The Lord is always revealing more. That is why the angels cry, "Holy! Holy! Holy!" God's love is without limit, and His faithfulness reaches the sky.

God's Anointing

If you want all that God the Father has planned for your life—to receive the total recovery anointing—you must ask for it in Jesus's name. The Spirit of God anoints your life for a very specific purpose: "*The Spirit of the Lord GOD is upon me; because the LORD hath anointed me to preach good tidings unto the meek; he hath sent me to bind up the brokenhearted, to proclaim liberty to the captives, and the opening of the prison to them that are bound*" (Isaiah 61:1).

God's Word declares that the anointing comes to bring restoration and recovery through your life, touching many:

> *To proclaim the acceptable year of the LORD, and the day of vengeance of our God; to comfort all that mourn; To appoint unto them that mourn in Zion, to give unto them beauty for ashes, the oil of joy for mourning, the garment of praise for the spirit of heaviness; that they might be called trees of righteousness, the planting of the LORD, that he might be glorified.* (Isaiah 61:2–3)

God's anointing is for you today. David certainly understood this, for the psalmist wrote, "*But my horn shalt thou exalt like the horn of an unicorn: I shall be anointed with fresh oil*" (Psalm 92:10).

Andrew Murray, a great revivalist of the late 1800s and early 1900s, stated, "At the moment of the new birth the Holy Spirit comes in and resides, yet His power is absent. It is not yet upon that life 'til that life surrenders to the one who is already there."[2]

The Holy Spirit comes in and dwells within your heart at the new birth, but after that it is your choice to surrender by giving Him your spirit, soul, and body. When you do, He empowers you.

Jesus said, *"He that believeth on me...out of his belly shall flow rivers of living water"* (John 7:38). He does not come upon you from heaven; He is already within. Andrew Murray described this in a beautiful picture as he spoke about a fountain coming from within you and literally baptizing you within itself.[3]

Imagine a fountain literally coming out of your belly, or heart (NKJV). You may not have even been aware that it was there until it comes out of you. The next thing you know, it surrounds you, immerseses you, and fills you to overflowing.

God's anointing for you will literally touch your life so deeply that even your expression will be affected. Psalm 104:15 says, "*Oil to make his face to shine.*" Symbolically, this speaks of your life being touched by God's tremendous love and shining again.

In his book *The Divine Conquest,* A. W. Tozer described this experience: "Nothing can take the place of the touch of God in the soul and the sense of Someone there."[4]

The anointing of God causes you to soar above the place that you have been. God's love for you is without measure, and His promise is that as you seek Him, you will find Him when you search for Him with all of your heart. God has promised to lift you from a low place and set your feet firmly upon high places. David wrote:

> *For thou wilt light my candle: the LORD my God will enlighten my darkness. For by thee I have run through a troop; and by my God have I leaped over a wall. As for God, his way is perfect: the word of the LORD is tried: he is a buckler to all those that trust in him. For who is God save the LORD? or who is a rock save our*

God? It is God that girdeth me with strength, and maketh my
way perfect. He maketh my feet like hinds' feet, and setteth me
upon my high places. (Psalm 18:28–33)

God's grace is sufficient for you, and His strength is made perfect in
your weakness. In His presence you will find all that you will ever need.

What is strength? It is the capacity for endurance and the power to
resist a force or attack. God will strengthen your life with His anointing
and take you from one high point to the next.

Did you know that God has even commanded strength toward you?
His anointing will cause you to go from weakness to great strength, from
lack to great abundance, from passivity to great power. God has commanded your strength: "*Thy God hath commanded thy strength: strengthen,*
O God, that which thou hast wrought for us" (Psalm 68:28).

A YIELDED VESSEL

All God needs is a surrendered container, someone who is willing to surrender and follow His call. In my life, I remember several low points
when I simply surrendered myself to God, and He touched me. With
one touch, He changed my life completely. I went from emptiness to the
most glorious experience in the Spirit. It is a learning process. All you
must do is welcome the Holy Spirit in your life and ask Him to draw you
closer to the Lord Jesus.

In *The Anointed Life*, Charles Spurgeon said:

> Look all through Scripture, and you will find continually
> that the will of man is described as being contrary to the
> things of God. What did Christ say to those who imagined
> that men would come to God without divine influence? He

said, first, *"No man can come to me, except the Father which hath sent me draw him"* (John 6:44).[5]

The Lord is about to do something mighty in your life, and all you must do is call upon His name. As you do, His anointing will flow down as fresh oil: *"For all the promises of God in him are yea, and in him Amen, unto the glory of God by us. Now he which stablisheth us with you in Christ, and hath anointed us, is God; Who hath also sealed us, and given the earnest of the Spirit in our hearts"* (2 Corinthians 1:20–22).

Every demon must flee when the anointing comes upon your life. God's promise is that your dry, parched ground shall become a pool of water:

> *Then shall the lame man leap as an hart, and the tongue of the dumb sing: for in the wilderness shall waters break out, and streams in the desert. And the parched ground shall become a pool, and the thirsty land springs of water: in the habitation of dragons, where each lay, shall be grass with reeds and rushes.* (Isaiah 35:6–7)

The Total Recovery Anointing

How do you experience God's overflow? The key is simply to come to Jesus. Peter understood this and that is why the anointing was so great upon his life that his very shadow carried God's healing presence.

I'll never forget a particular service in Pittsburgh where God filled my thirsty heart. I sat on the third row of the First Presbyterian Church worshiping the Lord as Kathryn Kuhlman began to minister to the people who were in attendance at the meeting, but I was so lost in the Spirit that I was unaware of what was happening around me.

I felt the Lord was closer to me than ever before. I also felt I needed to talk to the Lord but could only whisper, "Dear Jesus, please have mercy on me." Then I said again, "Jesus, please have mercy on me."

I felt so unworthy, like Isaiah when he entered the presence of the Lord and said, "*Woe is me! for I am undone; because I am a man of unclean lips*" (Isaiah 6:5). You cannot enter into the holy presence of the Lord without realizing your own filth and need of cleansing. And that is exactly what happened to me. It was as if a giant spotlight was beaming down on me. All I could see were my faults, weaknesses, and sins.

Again I said, "Dear Jesus, please have mercy on me." Then I heard a voice that I knew was the Lord. It was ever so gentle but unmistakably God speaking to me. He said, "My mercy is abundant on you." The words rang out in my ears: "My mercy is abundant on you."

I sat down and began sobbing and crying. There was nothing in my life to compare with the presence of the Lord I felt. His presence transforms our weakness to strength and our emptiness to fullness of joy. The Lord did it for me, and I know He can do it for you today if you will ask Him to.

Are you thirsty today? Do you need a touch from heaven? Do you want to walk in a greater anointing upon your life? Jesus said, "*If any man thirst, let him come unto me, and drink*" (John 7:37).

Jesus is the source. He alone can fill your life with all the fullness of God. The psalmist cried:

> *O God, thou art my God; early will I seek thee: my soul thirsteth for thee, my flesh longeth for thee in a dry and thirsty land, where no water is; To see thy power and thy glory, so as I have seen thee in the sanctuary. Because thy lovingkindness is better than life, my lips shall praise thee. Thus will I bless thee while I live: I will lift up my hands in thy name.* (Psalm 63:1–4)

As you go to the Lord in prayer today, your fellowship with God will increase, and He will draw you into a deeper, closer, and greater walk with Him, anointing you with a power that will help you live a life of total recovery!

A FINAL NOTE

My heart is so full, dear reader, for I have seen the Holy Spirit poured out in countries throughout the world. So many marvelous images of God's priceless anointing fill my thoughts. Each time I close my eyes, I can still see multitudes of beautiful faces filled with spiritual hunger in India, Panama, New York City, Nigeria, Philippines, Toronto, Japan, Mexico, and numerous other locations where we have held crusades throughout the world.

In each of these places, I've seen the Holy Spirit's oil pour over the multitudes, and I've watched as lives were touched by the precious Holy Spirit, never to be the same again. Granted, God may not be anointing you to be king of a nation as He did with David, but God desires for you to enter into His secret place and receive His anointing as David did. The Lord waits to fill you with His mighty power. All He needs is a willing vessel who will yield to Him.

Will you, as David did throughout his life, respond to His invitation today to be anointed by God's power? If so, why be satisfied with a drip of God's anointing on your life when you could have a river of oil dripping all over you?

When you are under the umbrella of God's power, you are in drive, not reverse. In Christ, you must go forward, not backward. He wants you to recover all, then move into a completely new dimension of power and anointing: *"I am come that they might have life, and that they might have it more abundantly"* (John 10:10).

The Christian life is an ever-expanding life, which moves from life into deeper life. The power of God causes the Christian life to be a journey of growth that continues to broaden outward and become a blessing to all it touches. It is like a light that goes out of one spot and moves in every direction.

As light expands (just as the universe is constantly in a state of expansion) we as Christians are continually increasing in life and growing. We go from life to doubled life, and then from doubled life to quadrupled life. As the power of God's multiplication touches life, it keeps expanding within the heart until it reaches abundant, unlimited life. From there, it continues to grow and expand until eventually it becomes life eternal.

The same principle applies to the anointing. As you remain in close fellowship with the Lord, the anointing will flow out of you. God wants you to experience His very best every day.

The glory of God and His marvelous presence will continue to expand within you as you remain in Him: "*But we all, with open face beholding as in a glass the glory of the Lord, are changed into the same image from glory to glory, even as by the Spirit of the Lord*" (2 Corinthians 3:18).

Glory will increase in your life as you behold the Lord and are affected by His presence. The process of growth continues until one day you are in eternal glory with the Lord. God wants you to be surrounded with increasingly abundant life, a life filled with anointing. David, as recorded in Psalm 23:5 declared, "*Thou anointest my head with oil; my cup runneth over.*"

Only in God's precious presence can this dimension of anointing and power descend down and cover you. As you run to God's everlasting arms today, you will find all you will ever need—and much more—to recover all!

This is my prayer for you.

9

TOTAL RECOVERY
FLOODGATES UNLEASHED

❖❖❖❖❖❖❖❖❖❖❖❖❖❖❖❖❖❖❖❖❖❖❖❖❖❖❖❖❖❖❖❖❖❖❖❖❖

And when David came to Ziklag, he sent of the spoil unto the elders
of Judah, even to his friends, saying Behold a present for you of the
spoil of the enemies of the LORD.

—1 SAMUEL 30:26

Total recovery means many things. To David, it meant safety, restoration, recovery, and ultimately abundance. Through praise, prayer, pursuit, and power, he and his band of 3-D followers were transformed into a powerful, prosperous nation.

One of the great reasons for David's triumph is no secret: he was a giver. David celebrated his victory through giving. The way in which he chose to distribute the spoils posed a sharp contrast to the way the Amalekites acted, using everything for their own lusts and pleasures.

David disposed of the spoils in a very different manner, choosing to distribute everything among his band of 600 men, not just the 400 who had accompanied him into battle, but even the 200 who had been left behind at the brook called Besor:

And David took all the flocks and the herds, which they drave
before those other cattle, and said, This is David's spoil. And

> *David came to the two hundred men, which were so faint that*
> *they could not follow David, whom they had made also to abide*
> *at the brook Besor: and they went forth to meet David, and to*
> *meet the people that were with him: and when David came*
> *near to the people, he saluted them.* (1 Samuel 30:20–21)

Some of David's soldiers were greedy and didn't want to share the spoil with those who remained behind, preferring to return only their wives and children, keeping the balance of the goods for themselves. David, however, was just and kind to those who remained behind, honoring them in the same way as those who had fought by his side when he penetrated the camp of the Amalekites and conquered them. David treated the 600 men the same by saying: "*For who will hearken unto you in this matter? But as his part is that goeth down to the battle, so shall his part be that tarrieth by the stuff: they shall part alike*" (1 Samuel 30:24).

It is interesting to note the details in the way David honored God as he dispersed the spoil, for he recognized that without God's help, he and his company of men would not have recovered the spoil nor prevailed over the Amalekites. He also demonstrated principles of wisdom and generosity that would make him an endearing king:

- He gave out of gratitude to God, acting as a good steward of everything that had been recovered.

- He gave in justice to his followers, dividing the spoil equally among the 600 men, recognizing that they had all been engaged in battle many times before and had done their part.

David didn't stop with his first acts of generosity: "*And when David came to Ziklag, he sent of the spoil unto the elders of Judah, even to his friends, saying, Behold a present for you of the spoil of the enemies of the* LORD*"* (1 Samuel 30:26).

David's story of total recovery began in Ziklag where everything was lost, and it ends with David coming back to Ziklag after recovering all. Apparently, he gave to people from whom he and his men had received assistance, intelligence, or provisions.

A very significant aspect of how David celebrated his victory is revealed in how he sent a portion of the spoils to others. Giving completed David's recovery.

David recovered his flocks, herds, cattle, and all his spoil. He not only recovered all, but he also took all of his enemy's possessions with him. Then he shared what was given. Upon that foundation, he began building a nation that would become prosperous and mighty. God's promise was fulfilled as *"there was nothing lacking to them…nor any thing that they had taken to them: David recovered all"* (1 Samuel 30:19). Everything that the enemy had stolen was recovered!

THE KEY

What if you were given a key and told it could unleash the greatest secrets of life? I want you to know that God offers a key to unlock the doors to power and wisdom, to abundance, debt-free living, and to a strong family heritage—to recover all!

Does that sound too good to be true?

David understood the key. Writing under the inspiration of the Holy Spirit, David explained the key: *"Give unto the* LORD *the glory due unto his name: bring an offering, and come into his courts. O worship the* LORD *in the beauty of holiness: fear before him, all the earth"* (Psalm 96:8–9).

The key is giving. It is not a gimmick. It is not the latest fad. It is simply God's principle that has worked since the beginning of time.

Today, many of the top corporate executives I have met understand this principle, even those who aren't grounded in the Word. They are generally givers. The same goes for the best political leaders and high achievers. Success and giving goes hand in hand.

The true secret, however, isn't just giving. It is giving according to God's plan. Look back at what David wrote in Psalm 96. Consider:

- **Giving gives God glory.** Every time you offer praise or tangible gifts, you give God glory. The Bible is filled with accounts of people who brought what they had in their hands—small or great—and were blessed with overwhelming abundance. That's not the reason to give though. Giving simply establishes authority and submission to God's plan for your life. It's a breakthrough moment when you finally realize what a giving heart does for your spiritual life. Giving brings openness to whatever God decides to do in an area of your life!

- **Giving enables you to come into God's presence properly.** Abraham understood this, according to Genesis 14, for he gave an offering to Melchizedek. This was four hundred years before the law was given to Moses, yet Abraham knew then what believers need to know today. To receive blessings from being in God's presence, you must come with an open, giving heart. The offering is tangible evidence of your inner desire. As we see in the Old Testament, a giving heart built a powerful legacy that moved from generation to generation, extending from Abraham to Isaac, Jacob, and beyond. There are certain steps to coming into God's courts. Giving enables you to do it properly.

- **Giving makes your worship complete.** It is recorded in the book of Numbers how Moses was given exact details for building the Tabernacle. Then he was commanded to tell the elders to bring offerings for specific times, and He outlined exact weights, amounts, and details. Granted, that was the law; today we are under grace, yet the principles remain the same. Giving is still part of our worship. Those who give freely are rewarded freely.

I have seen these principles proven in my own life over and over. Whenever you treat your giving as a mere exercise or something you *have* to do, the results are always less than satisfactory. But I have found that when I give with an open, fresh heart, I always receive accordingly.

Let me hasten to add that this isn't just about money. Far from it. These principles of giving are so vital and far-reaching because I sense a coming harvest unlike anything we've seen before. I want you to be aware of the crucial times in which we live, and I want you to understand the great key to success that will allow you to participate freely in the great outpouring beginning to happen.

Now is the time to get out of debt and unleash Isaiah 48:17 in your life: *"Thus saith the LORD, thy Redeemer, the Holy One of Israel, I am the LORD thy God which teacheth thee to profit, which leadeth thee by the way that thou shouldest go."*

God is ready to teach you how to give, how to profit, and how to establish a powerful heritage of giving in your family because giving is the key to success.

SUPERNATURAL BLESSINGS

David obviously knew that a supernatural law is activated by giving. We have just discussed what he wrote in Psalm 96. Psalm 112 also talks about activating God's blessing: *"He hath dispersed, he hath given to the poor; his righteousness endureth for ever; his horn shall be exalted with honour. The wicked shall see it, and be grieved; he shall gnash with his teeth, and melt away: the desire of the wicked shall perish"* (verses 9–10).

Blessings surround a giver. Malachi 3:10 is even more direct: *"Bring ye all the tithes into the storehouse, that there may be meat in mine house, and prove me now herewith, saith the LORD of hosts, if I will not open you the windows of heaven, and pour you out a blessing, that there shall not be room enough to receive it."*

Giving establishes your authority in God. David understood this principle, and that is why he gave. He had experienced too much loss already and didn't want to have to go back to the 3-D days.

God's Plan for Your Financial Recovery

God has a divine strategy and pattern for your financial success and restoration! The timeless keys to help you implement God's plan and to help you succeed are revealed throughout the Bible!

More than just formulas or some marketable infomercial "quick fix" to bring temporary relief to your situation, these scriptural principles for your financial success are eternal, fixed laws that cannot be changed. They must be observed by every believer and honored with the same reverence that David showed in front of his 3-D army.

The release of God's blessings in your life is connected to your obedi-ence, for the Bible declares: *"And all these blessings shall come on thee, and overtake thee, if thou shalt hearken unto the voice of the LORD thy God"* (Deuteronomy 28:2). In fact, obedience to God's Word is vital to your financial success, for the Bible declares: *"This book of the law shall not depart out of thy mouth; but thou shalt meditate therein day and night, that thou mayest observe to do according to all that is written therein: for then thou shalt make thy way prosperous, and then thou shalt have good success"* (Joshua 1:8).

As David showed by example, the success of your financial future is directly related to obeying God's laws of giving. God's divine plan for your financial success will not prevail without your cooperation! God's Word is clear, and you must obey God's command, which declares: *"Honour the LORD with thy substance, and with the firstfruits of all thine increase: So shall thy barns be filled with plenty, and thy presses shall burst out with new wine"* (Proverbs 3:9–10).

God wants to bless you in every area of your life, including your finances. There is no limit to God's supply, for His resources are inexhaustible: *"But my God shall supply all your need according to his riches in glory by Christ Jesus"* (Philippians 4:19).

As a special blessing, God's promise of increase is also extended to you and your children. *"The LORD shall increase you more and more, you and your children"* (Psalm 115:14).

God will teach you how to prosper: *"Thus saith the LORD, thy Redeemer, the Holy One of Israel, I am the LORD thy God which teacheth thee to profit"* (Isaiah 48:17).

God will bless the work of your hands. *"The LORD shall open unto thee his good treasure, the heaven to give the rain unto thy land in his season, and to bless all the work of thine hand: and thou shalt lend unto many nations, and thou shalt not borrow"* (Deuteronomy 28:12).

God will empower you to succeed. *"But thou shalt remember the LORD thy God: for it is he that giveth thee power to get wealth, that he may establish his covenant which he sware unto thy fathers, as it is this day"* (Deuteronomy 8:18).

God will meet your needs as you seek Him. *"The young lions do lack, and suffer hunger: but they that seek the LORD shall not want any good thing"* (Psalm 34:10).

God will bless and prosper you and your children when you fear and obey Him. *"Blessed is the man that feareth the LORD, that delighteth greatly in his commandments. His seed shall be mighty upon earth: the generation of the upright shall be blessed. Wealth and riches shall be in his house"* (Psalm 112:1–3).

God's blessings for you are always good. *"The blessing of the LORD, it maketh rich, and he addeth no sorrow with it"* (Proverbs 10:22).

God will bless your faithfulness: *"A faithful man shall abound with blessings"* (Proverbs 28:20).

God will meet your needs when you give to others in need. There will be no lack. *"He that giveth unto the poor shall not lack"* (Proverbs 28:27).

God will pour out His abundant blessings on you when you give cheerfully from a generous heart: *"But this I say, He which soweth sparingly shall reap also sparingly; and he which soweth bountifully shall reap also bountifully. Every man according as he purposeth in his heart, so let him give; not grudgingly, or of necessity: for God loveth a cheerful giver"* (2 Corinthians 9:6–7).

You can release God's abundant blessings on your life starting today as you obey God in the area of giving.

SEED-FAITH INSTRUCTION FROM ORAL ROBERTS

Several years ago I began to experience a new dimension of God's blessing in my own life when my dear friend Dr. Oral Roberts lovingly took the time to share his insights with me on the principles of sowing and reaping. What he communicated to me that day following a Sunday morning service at our church in Orlando revolutionized my perspective on giving and brought great blessings to my life, including my finances.

In the comfort of my office, Dr. Roberts began the conversation by saying, "Can I talk to you like a son?"

I responded affirmatively, eager to hear what he had to say.

"You take lousy offerings!" he said.

Stunned and surprised, I asked, "What do you mean, Dr. Roberts?"

"You ask the people to give, but you never tell them to expect a harvest. When a farmer sows, he does so expecting a harvest. When the grain is ripe and ready to harvest, a portion of the seed is planted for the next harvest, while the balance is used to provide for his needs. This morning when you asked the people to give, you told them what the Bible said and challenged them to give. But you never told them to expect a harvest!"

As I sat there listening to every word, Dr. Roberts continued to speak. "Sowing and reaping go together. I've never known a farmer who planted seed without expecting to reap a harvest!"

Next, Dr. Roberts began to quote a familiar verse from Luke 6:38, which declares: *"Give, and it shall be given unto you; good measure, pressed down, and shaken together, and running over, shall men give into your bosom. For with the same measure that ye mete withal it shall be measured to you again."*

Then Dr. Roberts pointed out that according to this verse, giving is referred to once. Yet, the blessing that comes from the act of giving is referred to seven times:

- *It shall be given*
- *unto you*
- *good measure*
- *pressed down*
- *shaken together*
- *running over*
- *shall men give into your bosom.*

These God-promised blessings that come as a result of giving are so abundant that your hand cannot contain it. The harvest can only be carried by balancing it against the chest with both arms stretched out as far as possible to grasp it and carry it home!

God Almighty is ready to release His blessings upon your life. Sow your seed today in faith and obedience, then expect your harvest so you can give again and again. When you are blessed, your needs are met, and you have no lack, then you can fulfill God's divine plan for your financial success as you become a living example of God's blessings.

Proverbs 28:20 says, *"A faithful man shall abound with blessings."* You cannot outgive God. He will always give you richer blessings and things that money cannot buy. As you remain faithful, as David did by giving to complete his recovery, God will keep blessing your life.

God created you to have good success, to subdue your enemies, and to attain His promises. The Lord will be faithful to restore all to you as you walk with Him, just as He restored all to David.

A FINAL WORD:
TOTAL RECOVERY AND YOU

Now there was long war between the house of Saul and the house of David: but David waxed stronger and stronger, and the house of Saul waxed weaker and weaker.

—2 Samuel 3:1

Total recovery means many things. To David, it meant safety, restoration, recovery, and ultimately abundance. Through praise, prayer, pursuit, and power, he and his band of 3-D followers were transformed into a powerful, prosperous nation. David's total recovery was just the beginning.

So it is with us. Our great commission as believers in Jesus Christ is to take the mighty message of the Gospel into all the earth. We are to share it with all nations, *"baptizing them in the name of the Father, and of the Son, and of the Holy Ghost"* (Matthew 28:19) and teaching them to observe the Lord's commandments.

Matthew 28:20 continues: *"I am with you always, even unto the end of the world."* The Lord Jesus is counting on you and me to go and tell others about His love, for the Lord knows that when His church truly fulfills the Great Commission, widespread recovery and revival will come.

Revelation 12:11 clarifies: *"And they overcame him by the blood of the Lamb, and by the word of their testimony; and they loved not their lives unto the death."* Your testimony and the knowledge of what the Lord Jesus has done for you can point many others toward salvation and total recovery. As you share the truth that God has put in your heart, it will bring souls out of darkness and into light, out of bondage and into the liberty of Christ.

There is a greater, eternal purpose for everything God does in your life—past, present, and future!

A New Season

God needs strong believers who understand the principle of total recovery. Something is happening that will shake the world to its very foundation. As discussed in chapter 8, God is beginning to release an anointing of His power that has never been experienced. The coming outpouring can only be described as being "without measure." To this point, what we have received has a dimension that allows us to measure and compare. Yet on the horizon is an anointing as immeasurable as the universe. It will be given to those who have been faithful with what they have already received. Jesus said: *"He that is faithful in that which is least is faithful also in much"* (Luke 16:10).

Every outpouring that comes from the Father is released as part of His master plan. It comes only in His timing. And I believe we are on the brink of God's greatest blessing, an unprecedented outpouring. As Paul shared in 2 Corinthians 3:18, *"But we all, with open face beholding as in a glass the glory of the Lord, are changed into the same image from glory to glory, even as by the Spirit of the Lord."* One total-recovery victory must become the foundation for another total-recovery victory. We are being prepared to move from glory to glory.

I must tell you that I'm so excited about what I'm hearing from the Father, for I believe a new day is here. A new wind is blowing! It is a new season in the spirit.

I believe with all my heart that God Almighty is taking our ministry to a new level. I not only believe it, but I can almost taste it. He is bringing us to a place where we're going to be affecting more lives and more souls than ever before. The impact will be seen in the number of people accepting Jesus Christ as Savior as well as in the incredible increase in the number of miracles.

Greater Impact

God has continued giving us more and more impact. When this ministry started nearly three decades ago, there were salvations, healings, and miracles much the same as now. The atmosphere was pretty much the same back then. The main thing that has changed is the size and impact.

Now we are going to see a higher plateau. We are moving into a new season where we will be seeing a much wider worldwide audience through our television programs. We will be going into larger arenas and coliseums, even for youth services. Already we are turning away thousands in many of the crusades, simply because the response has been more and more overwhelming. And I believe we're just getting a foretaste of what God has in store for us!

Entire nations impacted! That's a picture of what is to come. God Almighty is going to reveal what has been hidden from view. We are already beginning to see glimpses of what is coming.

We are living in a time that the saints have prayed for since Christ ascended to heaven. And what the Lord said in the last chapter of Mark is about to happen on an unprecedented scale, *"These signs shall follow them that believe"* (Mark 16:17). The demonstration of God's power will be flowing like a rushing, mighty river. The mighty army of Spirit-filled believers has already grown to untold millions, and we are just beginning to see the power of God multiplying as the promise is being fulfilled.

Jesus told His disciples: *"Heal the sick, cleanse the lepers, raise the dead, cast out devils: freely ye have received, freely give"* (Matthew 10:8) He gave them power over the enemy and said, *"Upon this rock I will build my church; and the gates of hell shall not prevail against it"* (Matthew 16:18).

And what Jesus proclaimed two thousand years ago is about to sweep across this world as never before, with might and power as more and more people grasp the principles of total recovery. And you can be part of it!

A Hunger for Greater Anointing

The ministry of Kathryn Kuhlman had a great impact on my life as a young minister. I can still recall how the auditoriums would explode with the presence of the Lord as Kathryn walked onto the stage. There was an instantaneous change in the atmosphere as the presence of God blew in with hurricane-like intensity.

A divine hunger for that anointing took hold of my being and caused me to seek the Lord with my whole heart. That hunger is one of the main reasons why God began touching my life in such a dynamic way. In this atmosphere of anointing, my ministry began to unfold.

Today I hunger more than ever for God's anointing. It is what keeps me in the Word. It is why I read books about John Wesley, Dwight L. Moody, Charles Finney, John G. Lake, and other great ministers of destiny. It's why I'm so conscientious about spending time with the Lord. Each of us needs fresh oil to be poured out every day by the Holy Spirit, especially as we prepare for exciting days to come.

I believe a greater anointing from the Holy Spirit is upon us as we seek more and more of Him and as we move into the deeper dimension of total recovery. What tomorrow holds will surpass anything man can perceive or fathom: *"Eye hath not seen, nor ear heard, neither have entered into the heart of man, the things which God hath prepared for them that love him. But God hath revealed them unto us by his Spirit: for the Spirit searcheth all things, yea, the deep things of God"* (1 Corinthians 2:9–10). Get ready for the coming "deep things" anointing!

A Deeper Prayer Life

The psalmist said, *"The LORD is near to all who call on Him, to all who call on Him in truth"* (Psalm 145:18, NKJV). David knew that the Lord does not respond to our prayers because of our excellent vocabulary or great knowledge. No! He pours out His precious and priceless anointing because He sees a heart that truly longs to know Him and is willing to act on that longing.

On the Day of Pentecost *"suddenly there came a sound from heaven as of a rushing mighty wind, and it filled all the house where they were sitting"* (Acts 2:2). Something occurred before that event that is often over-looked. The 120 believers gathered in the Upper Room to earnestly pray that the promised power of the Holy Spirit would descend. And as they prayed, the power came!

Earlier, when Jesus taught concerning prayer, He said that to receive the Holy Spirit we must ask. He said, *"If you then, being evil, know how to give good gifts to your children, how much more will your heavenly Father give the Holy Spirit to those who ask Him!"* (Luke 11:13, NKJV).

Peter and John experienced the power of the Holy Spirit as a result of prayer. They looked up to heaven and said: *"And grant unto thy servants, that with all boldness they may speak thy word, By stretching forth thine hand to heal; and that signs and wonders may be done by the name of thy holy child Jesus"* (Acts 4:30).

The Bible records what happens next: *"And when they had prayed, the place was shaken where they were assembled together; and they were all filled with the Holy Ghost, and they spake the word of God with boldness"* (Acts 4:31).

Deep prayer results in a visitation of the presence and power of God's Spirit. Anyone can pray, but praying with power comes only with the anointing of the Holy Spirit and with practice.

What would your life be like if you could move into the powerful, overwhelming, all-encompassing, eternal presence of God without fail, anytime you desired? How different would your life be? Your conversations? Your relationships? Your thoughts? Your goals? Your actions?

It is possible to enjoy the presence of God every day, to be ushered into the Holy of Holies! Only a relatively few people are in such a deep, close relationship with the Lord that the radiance from their encounters with God is evident to virtually everyone who comes in contact with them. Moses had to cover his face to keep from blinding the children of Israel. There was no mistaking the anointing on Elijah and Elisha. People knew when David was in the presence of God. More have followed throughout the Old and New Testaments, continuing to this day. Yet their numbers are few and far between.

I saw it happen with Kathryn Kuhlman. One time stands out in particular. I went with friends to her meetings in London, Ontario, and we stayed at a Holiday Inn. In the morning we walked into the hotel's restaurant to eat breakfast and started crying, not knowing why. Finally someone told us that Kathryn was staying in the hotel, too. I thought, "Now I know why I feel God's anointing in this place."

Later, I saw Kathryn walk out of an elevator and through the lobby. I didn't say anything to her. I was shaking. My whole body convulsed from head to toe. Jesus walked through that lobby with Kathryn Kuhlman. The place was stunned. The anointing settled on the place.

Although I cannot yet compare my own relationship with the Lord with that of such precious men and women of faith as those I've mentioned, I have known God in such an intimate way that I cannot describe His presence with words.

Early in my walk with the Lord, I spent an entire year with the Spirit of God so heavy on me. Imagine the most powerful anointing in one of our crusades, and that was what it was like for twelve months. At midnight, morning, anytime. It was overwhelming and constant. What a time it was! Then after a year, the anointing lessened in intensity, and I began a new phase of walking in faith. God allowed me to taste it, yet I believe if that anointing stayed that intense, I would not have been able to preach and minister as I do now. God put me on the mountaintop to understand what it was like; then I went to the valley to learn how to serve Him.

Through the ups and downs of the years since that time, I haven't known Him in such closeness all the time, of course. I can say, however, that God has shown me that He truly wants us to know Him as the priests did who were allowed in the Holy of Holies.

He wants every believer to walk in a deeper and deeper dimension of anointing. No matter what's going on in your life right now, be encouraged. There is hope. The question at this point is very simple: Are you willing to hunger and thirst for the presence of God? Are you willing to make your relationship with Him the most important part of your life? Are you willing to pay the price for such a wonderful union with Him.

Only a deep personal relationship can help us fulfill what God is calling us to do during this new season.

A Greater Understanding of the Word

Many people attempt to comprehend what God is doing in the world without intimately knowing the God of the Bible. Their minds may be filled with knowledge, yet they cannot understand what they have read because they don't seek Him diligently through His Word.

When a relationship is established, a revelation also grows. As evangelist Dwight L. Moody once said, "A Christian on his knees will see more than a philosopher on his tip toes."[1] Here's how:

- The Word reveals God to mankind.
- The Word provides the answers for every challenge we face.
- The Word brings God to earth and brings us into fellowship with Him.
- The Word reveals what will happen next.

One of the reasons David could lead his ragtag 3-D army to great power is clearly because he prayed earnestly for that dimension of understanding:

> *Oh, how I love thy law! it is my meditation all the day. Thou through thy commandments has made me wiser than mine enemies: for they are ever with me. I have more understanding than all my teachers: for thy testimonies are my meditation. I understand more than the ancients, because I keep thy precepts.* (Psalm 119:97–100)

The Lord stands ready to provide answers to our deepest desires: *"For I am the LORD: I will speak, and the word that I shall speak shall come to pass"* (Ezekiel 12:25), yet how can we know what God has in store for us during coming days unless we are willing to spend time in His Word seeking His wisdom and His knowledge? We learn in 2 Timothy 3:16: *"All scripture is given by inspiration of God, and is profitable for doctrine, for reproof, for correction, for instruction in righteousness."*

When we want to move into a deeper dimension of anointing, we must commit ourselves to knowing Him more. That knowledge and His wisdom, as well as a lifetime of total recovery, comes only through a diligent study of His Word.

UNDERSTANDING THE TIMES

In Matthew 24 the Lord was asked about the last days. Jesus said: "*And this gospel of the kingdom shall be preached in all the world for a witness unto all nations; and then shall the end come*" (verse 14).

We are coming closer and closer to the time of the Lord's return. Yet in the midst of some of the most uncertain and perilous times our world has known, God is opening unimaginable doors to the Gospel. What happens next, I believe, will be a direct result of how believers respond and how much they understand the importance of claiming total recovery.

It is up to each of us to get under the flow. Don't be a bystander as God does His work. When the Lord begins to pour out His blessing, stand beneath the flow and be drenched from head to toe.

It is astonishing to see what happened in the book of Acts. When Philip went to Samaria, the people saw the mighty power of God in action as never before. They were saved, baptized in water, and had great joy. The Bible says when the apostles came, they discovered that the Holy Spirit "*had fallen upon none of them. They had only been baptized in the name of the Lord Jesus*" (Acts 8:16, NKJV).

These people had seen the miracles, heard and believed the Word, and were even baptized, yet had never been touched by the Spirit. Peter and John arrived and "*laid their hands on them, and they received the Holy Ghost*" (Acts 8:17).

Likewise, the Lord wants each of us to move into a new dimension, to become enflamed and aglow with His Spirit. He desires that you come alive, more than ever before, by the touch of His mighty hand. Today, in this new season, you can experience God's presence as never before. Just as Elisha asked for a double portion of the Spirit then went forward in faith to be used as a powerful servant for the kingdom, you can be drenched and empowered to accomplish more in the coming days, months, and years than you ever dreamed.

I believe we have seen just a foretaste of the Holy Spirit's anointing. What comes next will be amazing. The ax head is rising, signaling a strengthening of God's power and a greater anointing. What awaits us on the horizon will be wonderful and breathtaking.

Get ready. It's a new season!

Your Season of Total Recovery

Take a few moments to consider what the enemy of your soul has stolen from you. What losses have been most painful and destructive?

What do you think your life will be like when God restores what the devil has tried to take from you? How will your life be different?

My prayer is that you will move more deeply into the principles of praise, prayer, pursuit, and power, and that God will begin helping you toward total recovery.

Now, let me pray a prayer of agreement with you:

God, I ask that we experience a new atmosphere of heaven today. Lord, I pray that all the enemy has stolen will be recovered. By Your Holy Spirit, I ask that You fill us with Your presence. Fuel

a greater desire to praise You and spend time with You in prayer. Give us strength, faith, and power as everything the enemy has stolen is taken back. Lord, may all be restored, and may all believers spend the coming days in abundance and service as we take the light of Your salvation to the world. In the mighty name of Jesus. Amen!

NOTES

Introduction: David's 3-D Army

1. Charles Finney, *The Spirit-Filled Life* (New Kensington, PA: Whitaker House, 1999), 117.

Chapter 1: God's Plan for Total Recovery

1. Charles Spurgeon, *Faith* (New Kensington, PA: Whitaker House, 1995), 63.

Chapter 2: Total Recovery Through Praise

1. Fenelon, *The Seeking Heart* (Jacksonville, FL: Seed Sowers, 1992), 14.
2. "God Leads Us Along." Words and music by George A. Young.
3. Author unknown, "When the Spirit of the Lord."
4. Dwight L. Moody, *Your Victory in Jesus* (New Kensington, PA: Whitaker House, 1995), 12.

Chapter 3: Total Recovery Through Prayer

1. R. A. Torrey, *The Power of Prayer* (New Kensington, PA: Whitaker House, 2000), 31–32.
2. Charles Finney, *Experiencing the Presence of God* (New Kensington, PA: Whitaker House, 2000), 194.
3. Andrew Murray, *Secrets of Authority* (New Kensington, PA: Whitaker House, 2002), 158.
4. Watchman Nee, *Spiritual Authority* (New York: Christian Fellowship Publishers, Inc. 1972), 167.
5. Smith Wigglesworth, *Smith Wigglesworth on Faith* (New Kensington, PA: Whitaker House, 1998), 175.

Chapter 4: Total Recovery Through Pursuit

1. Jeanne Guyon, *Experiencing the Depths of Jesus Christ* (Jacksonville, FL: Seed Sowers, 1975), 27.
2. E. M. Bounds, *Guide to Spiritual Warfare* (New Kensington, PA: Whitaker House, 1984), 147.
3. Wigglesworth, *Smith Wigglesworth on Faith*, 169.
4. Ibid., 135.
5. Ibid., 189.

Chapter 5: Total Recovery Through Power

1. Bounds, *Guide to Spiritual Warfare,* 148.
2. Nee, *Spiritual Authority,* 167.
3. Ibid., 43–44.

Chapter 7: Weapons of Total Recovery

1. Bounds, *Guide to Spiritual Warfare,* 152.
2. Ibid., 148.

Chapter 8: Your Anointing for Total Recovery

1. Smith Wigglesworth, *Experiencing God's Power Today* (New Kensington, PA: Whitaker House), 139.
2. Murray, *Secrets of Authority,* 158.
3. Ibid., 159.
4. A. W. Tozer, *The Divine Conquest* (Camp Hill, PA: Christian Publications, 1950, 1978), 43.
5. Charles Spurgeon, *The Anointed Life*, 192.

A Final Word: Total Recovery and You

1. Moody, *Your Victory in Jesus,* 12.